Harry's New York Bar
SANK ROO
DOE NOO

HARRY'S BAR

1911–2011

Isabelle MacElhone

KNESEBECK

VORWORT

Harry's Bar ist legendär und auch heute noch beliebt und gut besucht. Dieses Buch ist eine Chronik der Bar, ihrer Entstehung und Entwicklung und ihres phänomenalen Erfolgs.

Es ist an der Zeit, ihre Geschichte zu erzählen. Zwar wurden die Memoiren, die Harry MacElhone verfasst hatte, durch ein Feuer zerstört, aber zum Glück haben sich eine außergewöhnliche Sammlung von Fotos und Zeitungsausschnitten sowie zahlreiche Erinnerungen von Prominenten und Gästen erhalten, die bis zur Eröffnung der Bar im Jahr 1911 zurückreichen.

Als Anne Devanlay als erste Außenstehende einen Blick auf diese persönliche Sammlung aus dem Besitz der Familie MacElhone werfen durfte, überzeugte sie Andrew und Duncan MacElhone, Harrys Sohn und Enkel, die nacheinander die Bar geführt haben, deren einzigartige Geschichte und Tradition zu erzählen und ihre Schatztruhe mit Anekdoten über die Ereignisse aus all den Jahren für kommende Generationen zu öffnen.

Dieses Jahr wollen wir das hundertjährige Bestehen unseres Hauses feiern, indem wir unsere Historie mit Ihnen teilen. Doch die Geschichte von Harry's Bar ist damit noch lange nicht beendet. Während eine neue Generation das Ruder übernimmt, wird sie weitergeschrieben – dank neuer Freunde und der vielen treuen Stammgäste dieser einmaligen Institution, die dem Wandel der Mode und des Zeitgeists widerstanden hat.

Harry's Bar ist zwar geschichtsträchtig, aber kein Museum. Hier pulsiert das Leben von heute, ohne dass deshalb die Tradition verlorenginge, und vielleicht ist gerade das der Schlüssel für ihren Erfolg.

Wir danken unseren wundervollen Mitarbeitern, deren Professionalität, gemischt mit einem dezenten Schuss Humor und der Freude am Umgang mit Menschen, den besten Cocktail ergibt, den eine Bar nur bieten kann.

Cheers everybody!

Franz-Arthur und Isabelle MacElhone

PREFACE

Harry's Bar is a legendary watering hole that is still very much alive and thriving today. This book chronicles its history and its success.

The vivid history of Harry's Bar is a story waiting to be told. The memoirs penned by Harry MacElhone were destroyed by fire, but an outstanding collection of photos taken in the Bar, of newspaper clippings featuring it, and of numerous reminiscences by celebrities and nobodies has been scrupulously preserved since Harry's Bar opened in 1911.

This "personal collection" that the MacElhone family had never revealed before, has for the first time been made available to a great fan of Harry's Bar, Anne Devanlay. Anne convinced Andrew and Duncan MacElhone, Harry's son and grandson, who have successively presided over the Bar, to tell the history of this unique establishment, of its stories and traditions, and to recite for new generations the extraordinary lode of anecdotes about events that have taken place there through the years.

This year, we decided to commemorate the centennial of Harry's Bar by sharing our story with you.

As one generation takes over from the previous one, the chronicles of Harry's Bar are still being written, thanks to our customers and patrons, who are so attached to this unique venue, untouched by changing fashions.

Harry's Bar has plenty of history, but it isn't a museum. It's alive and vibrant, while never losing sight of its traditions. Perhaps that's what our regulars like about it.

We'd like to thank the wonderful staff at Harry's Bar, whose professionalism, mixed with a fine streak of good humour and an enormous love of human contact, makes the best cocktail you'll ever find in a bar.

Cheers everybody!

Franz-Arthur and Isabelle MacElhone

PRINCETON
DARTMOUTH
Melbourne Grammar
ST. BONAVENTURE
CAL STATE LA
COLBY
LEEDS UNIVERSITY
A.D. 1880.
DULWICH
A.D. 1619.
BRASENOSE (OXON)
A.D. 1512
ET AUGE BITUR
SCI-EN-TIA

UNIVERSITY OF SCRANTON
KENT STATE
KENT STATE UNIVERSITY OHIO 1910
CLEMSON
CAMPION
COLORADO
BLAIR
ELMHURST
COLLEGIUM ELMHURSTIENSE
BOURGOGNE
Monsieur Harry Mac Elhone
a été reconnu digne de faire partie de la Confrérie des
Chevaliers du Tastevin
Le Grand Chancelier
Le Grand-Maître de l'Ordre
GONVILLE & CAIUS (Cam.
A.D. 1348

HARRY'S BAR CUP
MORGINS
Harry's ABC of mixing cocktails
Harry MacElhone
I.B.F.
TRAP N°1
calvados
BUSNEL
Grande Fine Armagnac
JANNEAU
MARTELL
XO
MILWAUKEE
BANCO DE MEXICO
TEN POUNDS
The Royal Bank of Scotland plc
EASTERN CARIBBEAN
REAIS
BRASIL

THE UNITED STATES OF AMERICA
ONE DOLLAR
TWO DOLLARS
SEX DOLLARS
CENTRAL BANK OF THE ISLAMIC REPUBLIC OF IRAN
TEN THOUSAND RIALS
10000
250000
MARTELL
Hennessy
CHARTREUSE
MOUNT GAY RUM
Extra Old
BARBADOS RUM
OLMECA
TEQUILA
GOLD
J.BALLY
RHUM VIEUX
AGRICOLE
MARTINIQUE
1997
ABSINTHE
CANADA
MIKE C
FROM
MONTREAL

America's
Commando Parachutiste de l'air
30.566
TRY OUR H
CHIENS CHAUDS
STOP
BARTENDER
ABUSE!
OBAMA
BIDEN
CARTES
GRISES

OT DOGS
TOUTE HEU

HARRY MAC ELHONE

»Würde man alle Besucher von Harry's Bar in New York Schulter an Schulter in einer Reihe aufstellen – die Kette würde was weiß ich wohin reichen. Und könnte man die Menge an Alkohol abschätzen, die getrunken wurde, und die Flut der Worte, die gefallen sind, wäre das ein guter Einstieg in eine Geschichte dieses Lokals.«

Diese Zeilen vom 1. Juni 1934 stammen aus einem Artikel der *Chicago Daily News*. Damit war die Legende von Harry's Bar geboren. Die Zahl ihrer Freunde wuchs, und bald rannten die Leute Harry die Tür ein. Der Grund dafür war, dass es im Paris des frühen 20. Jahrhunderts nur wenige Bars im amerikanischen Stil gab, obwohl es an trinkfreudigen Amerikanern nicht mangelte. Und so wurde die Bar zu ihrer Stammkneipe, wie glücklich oder dramatisch die Zeiten auch waren.

Aber gehen wir zurück zu den wenig bekannten Anfängen von Harry's Bar.

"Suppose you took all the people who've been in Harry's New York Bar and lined them up, shoulder to shoulder. They would probably reach somewhere. Then if you could calculate the amount of alcohol consumed and the number of words spoken, you might have the beginning of a history of Harry's."

These lines, written on 1 June 1934, are taken from an article that ran in the *Chicago Daily News*, and the legend of Harry's Bar was born. More and more aficionados began beating a path to Harry's door, because there were few American-style cocktail bars in Paris in the early years of the 20th century, even though there was no shortage of Americans to patronize them. So whether the times were happy or dramatic, Harry's Bar became their watering hole of choice.

But let's first go back to the little-known origins of the Bar.

FROM **MANHATTAN** TO **PARIS**

VON **MANHATTAN** NACH **PARIS**

Tod Sloan war ein ehemaliger US-amerikanischer Jockey, der die geduckte Sitzposition für Galopprennen, die sogenannte »Monkey Crouch«-Position, erfunden hatte. Er beschloss im Jahre 1911, eine Bar in Paris zu eröffnen. Vom Geschäft verstand er nichts. Ein Freund namens Clancey, den er aus New York kannte, hatte eine Bar in Manhattan, um deren Fortbestand er sich angesichts der drohenden Prohibition in Amerika Sorgen machte. Neun Bundesstaaten hatten bereits den Alkoholkonsum verboten. Also schlug Tod Sloan Clancey vor, gemeinsam eine Bar in Paris aufzumachen, wo, rein theoretisch jedenfalls, keine Prohibitions-Gefahr drohte. Tods Plan sah vor, dass Clancey seine Bar in der Seventh Avenue komplett abbauen und in der Rue Daunou in Paris neu einrichten sollte. Das erwies sich als geniale Idee.

Die Rue Daunou ist nicht weit vom Ritz und dem Café de Paris entfernt, zwei wichtigen Touristentreffs. Und das Opéra-Viertel war schon damals beliebt bei amerikanischen Frauen, die es in die Modehäuser, Kaufhäuser und den Louvre zog. Tod Sloan war sicher, dass eine amerikanische Bar in dieser Gegend ein Riesenerfolg werden musste.

Und so wurden alsbald zwei Schwingtüren wie in den Saloons der Westernfilme in die Rue Daunou geliefert und mit ihnen eine prächtige Mahagoni-Bar, an der schon Generationen von Kneipengängern aus Manhattan gesessen hatten. Die Wände wurden mit Mahagoni getäfelt, die Decke wurde reich mit Arabesken verziert. Schließlich war alles so weit, und der künftig berühmteste Treffpunkt von Paris konnte seine Türen öffnen. Die »New York Bar«, die erste ihrer Art in Paris, die nicht in ein Hotel integriert war, war geboren.

Die Einweihung fand am 26. November 1911 zu Thanksgiving statt, dem wichtigsten Feiertag im amerikanischen Kalender. Zu diesem Zeitpunkt betrat auch Harry MacElhone die Bühne.

In 1911, Tod Sloan, a former US jockey famous for inventing the "monkey crouch" style of riding, decided to open a bar in Paris. He knew nothing about the business. One of his New York friends, a certain Clancey, owned a bar in Manhattan but was concerned about the survival of his establishment because of the looming threat of Prohibition in the United States. By that time, nine states had already banned the consumption of alcoholic beverages. As a result, Tod Sloan suggested he and Clancey go into business together and open up a bar in Paris, a city where, in theory, there would be no problem with Prohibition. Tod suggested that Clancey should completely dismantle his bar in New York and shift it from Seventh Avenue to 5, Rue Daunou, in Paris. Sheer genius!

Rue Daunou is close to the Ritz and the Café de Paris, two major tourist hangouts. The Opéra neighborhood was already very popular with American women, drawn to the couture houses, the department stores and the Louvre. Tod Sloan was sure that an American bar in that area would be a roaring success.

Two batwing doors, like those in saloons in Westerns, were accordingly delivered to Rue Daunou, along with a superb mahogany bar that had been polished by generations of Manhattan drinkers. The walls of the bar were covered in mahogany paneling, and the ceiling was decorated with embossed arabesques. When everything was ready, the doors finally opened at what was destined to become the most celebrated meeting place in Paris. The New York Bar – the capital's first American bar not in a hotel – was born. The inauguration took place on 26 November 1911, Thanksgiving: the most important holiday in the American calendar. It was at that point, too, that Harry MacElhone came on the scene.

1. Harry hinter der Theke im Ciro's in London / *Harry behind the counter at Ciro's in London*
2. Das Royal Hotel, Dundee / *The Royal Hotel, Dundee*

1.

HARRY THE ARTIST

HARRY **DER KÜNSTLER**

Harry MacElhone wurde am 16. Juni 1890 in Dundee in Schottland geboren. Sein Vater produzierte und vertrieb Sackleinen und erwartete, dass sein Sohn eines Tages das Familiengeschäft übernehmen würde. Harry aber träumte schon lange davon, in einer Bar zu arbeiten.

Er fand einen Job als Hilfskellner im Royal Hotel in Dundee, bevor er nach England zog und dort nacheinander in mehreren Hotels arbeitete. 1908 kam er an die französische Riviera, wo reiche Amerikaner einen Teil des Jahres verbrachten, von einer Party zur nächsten zogen und die Bars und Casinos bevölkerten. Harry wurde Barkeeper in den Casinos von Nizza und Cannes und schloss seine Ausbildung in den Heilbädern in Vittel, Aix-les-Bains und Enghien ab. Als er nach Paris kam, traf er Tod Sloan, der ihm einen Job in seiner New York Bar anbot.

Harry war sehr beliebt bei den Gästen, und bald verabredeten sich die Leute nicht mehr in der »New York Bar«, sondern in »Harry's Bar«. Dessen ungeachtet beschloss Harry, nach Amerika zu reisen, um aus erster Hand zu erfahren, wie Liebhaber alkoholischer Getränke ihre Cocktails brauten, servierten und genossen. 1912 kam er in New York an und übernahm die Bar im Plaza. Dort machte er sich mit den Trinkgewohnheiten der Amerikaner vertraut, ihrem Geschmack, Lebensstil und Sinn für Humor. Doch der Aufenthalt war eine Enttäuschung. Die gottesfürchtigen Puritaner, allen voran die Anti-Saloon-Liga, sowie weitere Gruppen traten energisch für die Durchsetzung der Prohibition in Amerika ein, da Alkohol in ihren Augen der Kern allen Übels einer dekadenten europäischen Gesellschaft war, das durch Italiener, Iren und andere Immigranten in die USA eingeschleppt wurde. Harry hatte bald genug von diesem »trockenen« Trend. Außerdem plagte ihn das Heimweh. Bei Ausbruch des Ersten Weltkrieges 1914 reiste er mit dem Schiff zurück nach Großbritannien, wo er sich zum Kriegsdienst meldete und dem Royal Naval Air Service (RNAS) beitrat.

Nach Kriegsende eröffnete er mehrere Bars in London, darunter den Buck's Club und den Hendon Flying Club, bevor er ins Savoy wechselte. Kurze Zeit später wurde er Chefbarkeeper im Ciro's, einer berühmten Bar in London. Harry war bald stadtbekannt. 1919 stieg sein Ruhm weiter, durch die Veröffentlichung eines Büchleins mit dem Titel *ABC of Mixing Cocktails*, das 300 Cocktail-Rezepte und jede Menge Tipps enthielt. Das Büchlein wird auch heute noch regelmäßig aktualisiert und ist ein Muss für jeden Cocktail-Liebhaber.

Es dauerte nicht lange und der Besitzer des Ciro's bot Harry MacElhone an, eine Ciro's-Filiale in Deauville aufzumachen.

2.

Harry MacElhone was born in Dundee, Scotland, on 16 June 1890. His father manufactured and sold hessian (burlap), and was sure his son would take over the family business. However, Harry himself had long dreamed of working behind a bar.

He found a job as a busboy at the Royal Hotel in Dundee. After that, he travelled south to England, where he worked in a succession of hotels. In 1908, he arrived on the French Riviera, where wealthy Americans would spend part of the year, going from party to party and from the bars to the casinos. Harry was hired as a barman at the casino in Nice and then at the casino in Cannes. To complete his training, he went to the spas at Vittel, Aix-les-Bains and Enghien. On returning to Paris, he met Tod Sloan, who offered him a job behind his bar.

Harry was very popular with the customers, and soon people were arranging to meet at "Harry's Bar" and not at the "New York Bar". Nevertheless, Harry decided that he needed to travel to the United States to see how those great fans of alcoholic beverages concocted, served and drank cocktails. Arriving in New York in 1912, he took over the bar in the Plaza. There, he observed Americans' drinking mores and customs, their tastes, their lifestyles and their sense of humor. But he was disappointed. Notably represented by the Anti-Saloon League, the country's God-fearing puritans and others were campaigning strenuously for the prohibition of liquor, which in their eyes was the evil at the heart of decadent European societies imported into the United States by Italian, Irish and other immigrants. Harry quickly tired of this "dry" trend. He was also homesick.

When the Great War broke out in 1914, Harry boarded a ship for Britain, where he enlisted and was commissioned into the Royal Naval Air Service (RNAS).

After the war ended, he opened a number of bars in London, such as the Buck's Club and the Hendon Flying Club, then went to work at the bar in the Savoy hotel. Shortly afterwards, he was hired as head barman at Ciro's, a famous London establishment, and rapidly became a very well-known figure in the city. In 1919, his fame was further boosted with the publication of a booklet entitled *ABC of Mixing Cocktails*, which contained 300 recipes for cocktails and lots of advice. (Continually updated, the manual is, even today, a must for cocktail lovers.)

Shortly thereafter, the owner of Ciro's asked Harry to launch a Deauville branch.

THE **NEW YORK BAR** BECOMES **HARRY'S BAR**

AUS DER **NEW YORK BAR** WIRD **HARRY'S BAR**

Nachdem Harry ein Jahrzehnt lang die besten Bars der Welt erkundet hatte, war die Zeit reif für ein eigenes Etablissement, eines, das dem Ruf gerecht werden würde, den er sich im Lauf der Jahre erarbeitet hatte. Hinzu kam, dass Harry gern zurück nach Paris wollte. 1923 ging sein Traum in Erfüllung: Die New York Bar stand zum Verkauf.

1913, zwei Jahre nach der Einweihung der Bar, die Tod Sloan von Manhattan nach Paris verschifft hatte, stand dieser wegen hoher Spielschulden vor dem Ruin. Er kehrte zurück in die Vereinigten Staaten und arbeitete dort als Rennpferdetrainer, was seiner wahren Leidenschaft entsprach. Die New York Bar verkaufte er an seinen Jockeykollegen Milton Henry, dessen Frau Nell in ganz New York bekannt war. Sie war auch ein großer Rennsportfan und verbrachte ihre Nachmittage meist auf der Rennbahn.

Bei Ausbruch des Krieges im Jahr 1914 verkauften Milton und Nell Henry die New York Bar an britische Investoren und zogen nach Hause in die USA.

In den Zwanzigerjahren, als es mit dem Pferderennsport weiterging, tauchte Nell wieder in Paris auf und kaufte die New York Bar zurück, diesmal jedoch mit einem neuen Ehemann an der Seite. Sie hatte einen New Yorker Börsenmakler geheiratet und trug nun den Namen Nell MacGee. Sie bezog ein Zimmer im Hotel Daunou, gleich gegenüber der Bar, und scharte nachmittags nach den Rennen an einem der hinteren Tische ihre Verehrer um sich. Doch nach einigen Jahren langweilte Nell das Pariser Gesellschaftsleben, und sie bot die Bar erneut zum Verkauf an.

Da erschien Harry erneut auf der Bildfläche. Das Geschäft zwischen ihm und Nell wurde am 8. Februar 1923 abgeschlossen. Harry stellte seinen eigenen Namen dem Schriftzug voran, und so entstand Harry's New York Bar, auf die noch weitere, schlicht Harry's Bar genannt, folgten. Am selben Tag wurde sein Sohn Andrew in London geboren. Die Zukunft des Neugeborenen wurde auch sogleich festgelegt, denn Andy sollte einmal die Bar übernehmen.

After a decade exploring the world's finest bars, Harry decided that it was now time to open his own establishment – one worthy of the reputation he had forged for himself over the years. And he wanted to see Paris again. In 1923, his dream at last came true: the New York Bar was up for sale.

In 1913, two years after the inauguration of the bar he had shipped from Manhattan to Paris, Tod Sloan had been ruined by his gambling debts. He returned to the United States, where he was offered employment as a trainer of racehorses – his real passion. At that point, the New York Bar was sold to another American jockey, Milton Henry, whose wife, Nell, was a larger-than-life New Yorker. She was also a fan of racing and spent her afternoons at the racecourse.

With the outbreak of hostilities in 1914, Milton and Nell Henry sold the New York Bar to a syndicate of British investors and soon sailed back to the United States. Nell reappeared in Paris in the 1920s as horse-racing resumed. She bought back the New York Bar, but this time with a new husband. She had re-married and was now Nell MacGee, wife of a New York stockbroker.

Still larger than life, she took a room in the Hotel Daunou (just across the road from the bar), and from a table at the rear of Harry's, she reigned supreme over a band of admirers who enjoyed her company and her eccentricities after an afternoon at the races. She wore diamonds on every finger, and their glitter dazzled her customers. But Nell got bored, and after a few years of Paris high life, she again put the bar up for sale.

Harry was back on the scene. The transaction was closed on 8 February 1923. An exultant Harry prefixed his own name to the sign, and the bar became Harry's New York Bar. The first Harry's Bar in history was born. Harry was doubly delighted, because that very same day, his second son, Andrew ("Andy"), was born in London. The newborn's destiny was also confirmed that day, as he would take over running the bar from his father.

WHY AN AMERICAN BAR IN PARIS?

WARUM EINE AMERIKANISCHE BAR IN PARIS?

Harry MacElhone, ein gebürtiger Schotte, führte nun also eine amerikanische Bar in Paris und war wild entschlossen, auch die Franzosen für Cocktails zu gewinnen.

Die ersten dieser Mixgetränke gab es in England. Das Wort selbst ist ein Slangbegriff aus dem 18. Jahrhundert und bezeichnete ursprünglich eine Kreuzung von Rennpferderassen. Rotwein und Port waren damals dem Adel und den Londoner Clubs vorbehalten, während die armen Leute Bier und Gin tranken. Gin ist ein Kornschnaps, der oft auf minderwertige Art und Weise gebrannt wurde. Er wurde in der Regel mit Wacholderbeeren und manchmal auch mit Koriander aromatisiert. Oft fügte man Zucker hinzu, damit er trinkbar und der raue Geschmack überdeckt wurde. Hin und wieder wurden auch andere Zutaten beigemengt. So entstand der Cocktail. Gin Tonic zum Beispiel wurde aus medizinischen Gründen erfunden, als Offiziere der britischen Kolonialarmee das Chinin, das sie zum Schutz gegen Malaria einnahmen, mit Gin streckten.

Im Januar 1920 trat der 18. Zusatzartikel zur Verfassung der Vereinigten Staaten in Kraft, der den Beginn der Prohibition einläutete. 13 Jahre lang, bis 1933, waren Herstellung, Verkauf und Transport von Alkohol verboten. Doch bald schon blühten Schwarzbrennerei und Schwarzhandel. Es war die Ära von Al Capone. Schmuggler waren nachts im ganzen Land unterwegs, benutzten Nebenstraßen und änderten ständig ihre Routen, um Straßensperren der Polizei und Hinterhalten von konkurrienden Banden zu entgehen. Ein hochentwickeltes Vertriebsnetz entstand, um die geheimen Bars, die sogenannten Flüsterkneipen, mit Hochprozentigem zu versorgen. Dort wurde der gepanschte Alkohol zu astronomischen Preisen in Teetassen verkauft. Die Barkeeper dachten sich immer neue Rezepte aus und mischten ihn mit Fruchtsaft, Sirup und weiteren Zutaten, sowohl um den Alkoholgehalt der Getränke zu verschleiern als auch den bitteren Geschmack der minderwertigen Spirituosen zu überdecken.

Während viele Amerikaner in diese illegalen Saloons strömten, zogen andere ein »feuchtes« Wochenende auf Kuba vor, wo der Alkoholgenuss gesetzlich erlaubt war. Diejenigen, die es sich leisten konnten, emigrierten für eine Weile nach Frankreich, das vielleicht nicht für seine Spirituosen, wohl aber für seinen Wein berühmt war.

Harry MacElhone wusste sofort, wie er diese spezielle Klientel anlocken konnte, und bald wurde Harry's New York Bar der Treffpunkt schlechthin für Amerikaner in Paris, ob sie nun auf der Durchreise oder dort zu Hause waren. Harry war unglaublich erfinderisch und hatte ein untrügliches Gespür dafür, welche Atmosphäre den amerikanischen Barbesuchern zusagte. Diese Institution am rechten Seine-Ufer hielt sogar der »kulturellen Revolution« jener Zeit stand, die am linken Ufer Einzug hielt – erst in Montparnasse und dann in Saint-Germain-des Prés trafen sich die jungen Rebellen.

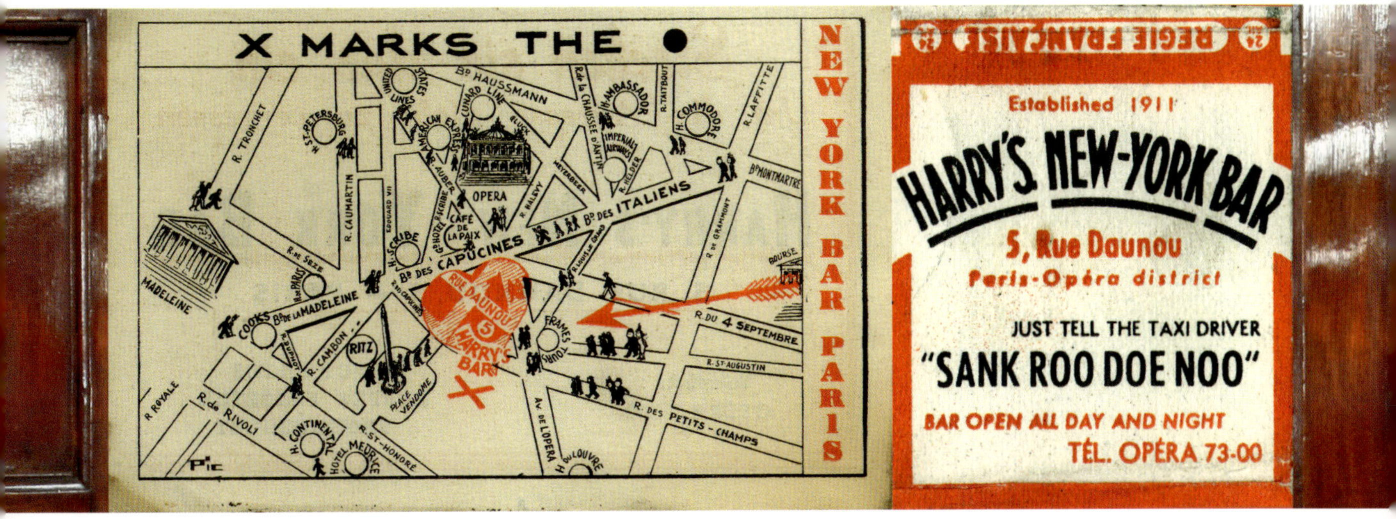

Harry MacElhone, a Scot by birth, now found himself running an American *cocktail bar* in Paris and was hell-bent on getting the French to start drinking cocktails.

The first cocktails were served in England. The word apparently derives from 18th-century slang for a cross-breed racehorse. In those days, claret and port were the preserve of the aristocrat and the London club. The poor drank beer and gin. Gin is a grain spirit that is distilled in rudimentary fashion, giving it a cloudy appearance. It was frequently flavored with juniper berries and sometimes by the addition of coriander. Often it was necessary to add sugar to make it drinkable, and to mask the taste. Occasionally, other things were added: enter the cocktail.

In the case of the Gin & Tonic, its source is medically-inspired: it was created by officers in the colonial army, who used gin to dilute the quinine that was necessary to protect them from malaria.

In January 1920, the Eighteenth Amendment to the United States Constitution came into force, marking the start of Prohibition, which lasted over a dozen years. Until 1933, the manufacture, sale and transport of alcohol were banned, but very soon a contraband system evolved. This was the Al Capone era. Bootleggers criss-crossed the country by night, constantly changing back roads to avoid police roadblocks and ambushes by other gangs. A full-fledged distribution network came into being to supply speakeasies. The adulterated spirits sold there at astronomical prices were often served in teacups. Barmen would then rack their brains to come up with recipes and mixed them with fruit juice, syrups or other ingredients, as much to hide the degree of alcohol as to mask the bitter taste of the poor-quality spirits.

While large numbers of Americans flooded into these new-style saloons, others preferred to go off and spend "wet" weekends in Cuba, where there were no legal restrictions whatsoever on the consumption of alcohol. Other, wealthier, drinkers emigrated for a while to France, which was famous, if not for its spirits, then for its wines.

Harry MacElhone knew instantly how to attract this particular class of drinker to his establishment, and Harry's New York Bar very soon became *the* meeting place for Americans, whether tourists or residents. The incredibly imaginative Harry had the knack of knowing how to recreate the atmosphere and mood that American drinkers loved. And this Right-Bank institution held out against the "cultural revolution" of the time, which was taking up residence on the Left Bank – during the Roaring Twenties in Montparnasse, and then subsequently in Saint-Germain-des-Prés, which was to be the scene for the "rebels without a cause" of the day.

THE ROARING TWENTIES

DIE WILDEN ZWANZIGER

1922 entstand allmählich das Amerika, das man mit dem amerikanischen Traum verbindet.

Paris erlebte zu dieser Zeit den Beginn einer großen kulturellen Revolution. Unmittelbar nach dem Ersten Weltkrieg erlangte die Stadt ihre internationale Bedeutung zurück und wurde erneut zum europäischen Schmelztiegel der Kulturen.

Amerika wurde für Paris zu einer Art Kultobjekt, das im Orbit der französischen Metropole kreiste. Die Menschen waren fasziniert von Hollywood, und die Intellektuellen fühlten sich am Puls des Zeitgeists. Wo man auch hinkam, jeder ließ sich mitreißen vom Jazz und seinem wilden Rhythmus. Es war die Ära der »Harlem Renaissance« und Josephine Bakers, der Hohepriesterin für Musik und Tanz in Paris.

Der Genuss von Cocktails wurde in dieser Zeit immer beliebter. Die Bohème in Montparnasse hatte eine ausgeprägte Vorliebe für Hochprozentiges, die Exil-Amerikaner demonstrierten gern, dass sie auf das Alkoholverbot in ihrer Heimat pfiffen, und die Franzosen zeigten sich nach den Entbehrungen der Kriegszeit ausgelassen und lebenshungrig. 1924 wurde die erste amerikanische Bar auf dem Montparnasse namens Select eingeweiht. Le Dôme, La Rotonde und die Closerie des Lilas folgten kurze Zeit später.

Das rechte Ufer hielt dem Ansturm des linken hartnäckig stand. Luxusrestaurants wie das Maxim's und Voisin und Bars wie Harry's Bar bewirteten auch diese neue Generation, die das Leben in etwas »gehobenerem« Ambiente genießen wollte als in Montparnasse. Am rechten Seineufer lockten die großen und exklusiven Modehäuser, die Juweliere am Place Vendôme, der Louvre, die Kunstgalerien der Rue de Rivoli und die großen Kaufhäuser. Hier erwarteten die Gäste einen Service, wie er in Amerika üblich war. Daher wusste auch jeder Barkeeper in Harry's Bar, wie man einen ordentlichen trockenen *Martini* macht.

In 1922, the America of the American Dream was beginning to emerge. Paris at that time was in the throes of a major artistic revolution. In the immediate aftermath of WWI, the city was restored to its international role. It was once again the melting pot of European cultural influences.

America was the cult object floating in the atmosphere. Hollywood and its cinema fascinated people and intellectuals were well aware of the zeitgeist. Everywhere, people were carried along by the crazy rhythms of jazz. This was the era of the "Harlem Renaissance", and of Josephine Baker, who officiated as high priestess of music and dance in Paris.

Cocktails were becoming increasingly popular. The Bohemian existence of the artists in Montparnasse owed much to a penchant for strong drink. American exiles liked to "cock a snook" at the alcoholic lockdown of Prohibition in their home country, while the French were starting to let their hair down following their wartime privations. In 1924, the Select, the first American bar in Montparnasse, was inaugurated. Le Dôme, La Rotonde and the Closerie des Lilas followed shortly thereafter.

The Right Bank fiercely resisted the Left Bank challenge. Luxury restaurants such as Maxim's and Voisin, and bars like Harry's Bar, also welcomed this new generation who wanted to enjoy life, but in more "upscale" surroundings than those of Montparnasse. On the Right Bank, people were attracted by the great couture houses, the jewelers of Place Vendôme, the Louvre, the art galleries of the Rue de Rivoli and the great department stores. Patrons expected a level of service identical to that found in the United States. At Harry's Bar, every barman knew how to prepare a Dry Martini properly.

Harry's Bar®
The oldest cocktail bar in Europe ™
1911 Sank Roo Doe Noo
3,50€
Harry's Pick-me-up*
Grenadine
orange juice
Cognac
Grand marnier
Champagne
Celebration
100 years
AIRBORNE
TRY OUR
CHIENS CHAU
STOP BARTENDER ABUSE!

Home of the "Internat
ROYAL WINNIPEG RIFLES CANADA
КЫРГЫЗСТАН
HOT DOGS
S À TOUTE HE

GUIDED **TOUR**

FÜHRUNG **DURCH DIE BAR**

Ganz allmählich verfeinerte Harry MacElhone die Einrichtung der Bar, die bis zum heutigen Tag so gut wie unverändert ist.

Die Banner amerikanischer und britischer Eliteuniversitäten schmücken die Wände ebenso wie die Wimpeln amerikanischer Footballteams, dazu eine Reihe von Karikaturen aus den Federn von Sem[1] und Toulouse-Lautrec, die Persönlichkeiten der Pariser Gesellschaft in den Zwischenkriegsjahren zeigen.

Auf dem Spiegel hinter der Bar ist das Emblem der International Bar Fly (IBF) abgebildet: zwei Fliegen in Abendgarderobe, die sich voreinander verbeugen. Die gekreuzten Schläger der finnischen Eishockey-Nationalmannschaft über dem Spiegel sind ein Symbol für die Sportbegeisterung, die in der Bar herrscht. An der Wand links neben dem Spiegel hängen Banknoten aus aller Welt, manche mit Widmungen, und gleich daneben Geldscheine aus der Kriegszeit. Harry hatte außerdem Artikel aus Zeitungen und Magazinen an die Wand gepinnt, in denen die Bar erwähnt wird. Einige davon haben sich im Privatarchiv der Bar erhalten.

Gleich über der Theke hängt ein kleiner Affe, dazu ein Hufeisen, ein Paar Boxhandschuhe, und einige Baseball-Bälle gibt es ebenfalls. Die Gäste glauben, dass es Glück bringt, diese Gegenstände anzufassen. Das Hufeisen stammt von *Man o' War*, einem der erfolgreichsten amerikanischen Vollblut-Rennpferde aller Zeiten. Die Boxhandschuhe hat Primo Carnera getragen, als er 1933 den Weltmeistertitel im Schwergewichtsboxen gegen Jack Sharkey durch K.o. gewann. Die White Sox und die Giants haben die von den Spielern signierten Baseball-Bälle gestiftet, als sie die Bar 1924, im Jahr ihrer »European Junket«-Tour besuchten.

Im Licht der letzten noch verbliebenen Gaslampe führt eine Treppe nach unten in eine etwas intimere Pianobar, die nur am Abend geöffnet ist. Von 1933 an hieß sie auch *Front-Page Cabaret*, weil sie mit Titelseiten von Zeitungen aus aller Welt tapeziert worden war. Dort wurde zur Pianomusik ausschließlich Champagner serviert.

1. Georges Goursat, genannt Sem (1863–1934), Grafiker, Karikaturist und Klatschkolumnist.

Very gradually, Harry MacElhone refined the décor of his bar, which remains virtually unchanged to this day.

Painted on wooden shields, the flags of top American universities and British university colleges were hung on the walls, alongside pennants of American football teams. There was also a series of caricatures by Sem[1] and Toulouse-Lautrec featuring leading lights of Paris society between the wars.

On the mirror behind the bar, the emblem of the International Bar Fly (I.B.F.): two flies in evening dress are bowing to each other. Above the mirror, the crossed sticks of the Finnish national hockey team point to the Bar's resolutely sporting spirit. On the wall to the left of the mirror, a collection of banknotes from all over the world, some of them with dedications, rubs shoulders with "war money" banknotes. Harry also posted newspaper and magazine articles mentioning Harry's Bar on the walls. Many of these are no longer there, as newsprint ages badly; many others have been preserved in the Bar's private archive.

Just above the bar hangs a small monkey along with a horseshoe, a pair of boxing gloves and some baseballs. Customers know that it's lucky to touch these objects. The horseshoe belonged to one of the greatest American Thoroughbred racehorses of all time, Man o' War. The boxing gloves are those worn by Primo Carnera in 1933, when he won the World Heavyweight championship against Jack Sharkey by a knockout. The White Sox and Giants donated the baseballs, and the players autographed them when they visited the bar in 1924, the year of the "European Junket" tour.

Under the last surviving gaslight, a staircase descends to the more intimate space of the piano-bar, open only in the evenings. From 1933 onwards, it was known as the Front-Page Cabaret, as it was papered with the front pages of newspapers from all over the world. Only champagne was served, to the accompaniment of the piano music.

1. Georges Goursat, aka Sem (1863–1934), poster artist, caricaturist and gossip columnist.

Eine Anzahl bedeutender Jazzmusiker probte dort unten, so Tommy Lyman, und jahrelang traten Leo Deslys und Roy Barton als Duo auf. An ebenjenem Piano im Souterrain komponierte auch ein gewisser George Gershwin sein Stück *Ein Amerikaner in Paris*, sehr zum Leidwesen der Gäste, denen die Akkorde und Dissonanzen, die seinem Schöpfergeist entsprangen, gar nicht gefielen. Einige boten sogar an, einen Klavierstimmer zu bezahlen, als sie Gershwin bei der Arbeit an seiner Komposition hörten. Er zeichnete die Noten auf Papierservietten auf. Leider wurden diese unbezahlbaren Autographe während des Krieges zum Befeuern des Ofens verwendet.

Auch wenn Harry's Bar schon allein durch das Dekor zu einer nahezu rein amerikanischen Einrichtung wurde, lag es doch an Harry MacElhones unverwechselbarer Persönlichkeit, dass der Bar ein so großer Erfolg beschieden war. Atmosphäre wie Cocktails waren gleichermaßen geprägt von seiner ungezwungenen, herzlichen Art. Er wurde nie müde, seine Gäste auf immer neue Weise zu unterhalten.

Harry hatte schon ein Gespür für Marketing, bevor der Begriff überhaupt erfunden wurde, und nahm jede Gelegenheit wahr, seine Bar in die Presse zu bringen. Natürlich achtete er auf den Umsatz, doch in erster Linie sollte seine Bar ein Ort sein, an dem Menschen einen entspannten Umgang miteinander pflegen konnten. Harry war immer da, um seine Gäste zu begrüßen. Er war sowohl eloquent als auch ein guter Zuhörer und hatte ein Gespür für Stimmungen der Menschen. Viele wurden Freunde, noch ehe sie Gäste waren. Er saß immer am selben Platz, gleich links neben dem Eingang, sodass er jeden willkommen heißen konnte. Sein freundliches Gesicht und seine Jovialität sind untrennbar mit dem Image der Bar verbunden. Man kannte ihn als kleinen, rundlichen Mann mit kurzgeschorenem Haar und buschigen schwarzen Augenbrauen.

Am 3. Juni 1958 starb Harry MacElhone an einem Herzinfarkt. Seinem Wunsch gemäß blieb die Bar geöffnet. Der Mann, der sein Leben lang anderen Menschen Freude spenden wollte, hatte sich eineTodesanzeige verbeten. Dennoch kamen alle Barkeeper aus Paris, um dem »alten Harry« die letzte Ehre zu erweisen. Von diesem Tag an nahm Andrew MacElhone den Platz seines Vaters ein. In Nachrufen hieß es: »gebürtiger Schotte, den man fälschlich für einen Amerikaner hielt, und Barkeeper mit ganzer Seele«[2], »bekannt von Paris bis San Francisco und London bis Singapur«[3], und ein Journalist stellte fest: »Die Vereinigten Staaten haben ihren berühmtesten Botschafter in Paris verloren.«[4] Dazu ergänzte Andrew: »Wir erzählten den Gästen jahrelang, dass er nur im Hinterzimmer sei und bald wiederkomme.« Auch heute noch ist Harrys Geist in der Bar gegenwärtig.

2. *Daily Mail*, 5. Juni 1958.
3. *Evening News*, 4. Juni 1958.
4. *Le Journal du dimanche*, 8. Juni 1958.

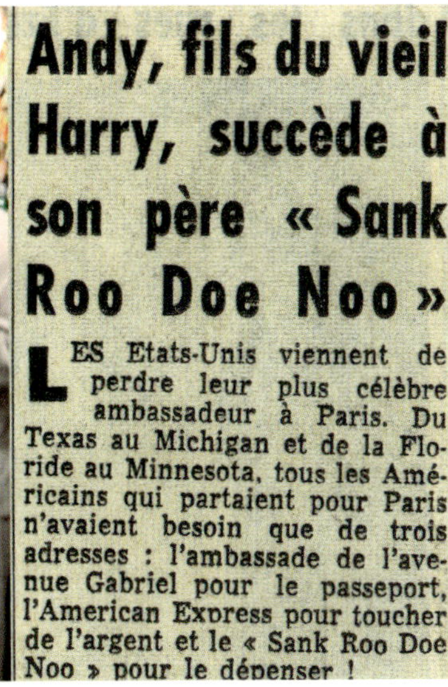

Andy, fils du vieil Harry, succède à son père « Sank Roo Doe Noo »

LES Etats-Unis viennent de perdre leur plus célèbre ambassadeur à Paris. Du Texas au Michigan et de la Floride au Minnesota, tous les Américains qui partaient pour Paris n'avaient besoin que de trois adresses : l'ambassade de l'avenue Gabriel pour le passeport, l'American Express pour toucher de l'argent et le « Sank Roo Doe Noo » pour le dépenser !

A number of leading jazzmen practiced there, including Tommy Lyman. For many years, Leo Deslys and Roy Barton performed in Harry's Bar as a duo. On that same piano a certain George Gershwin composed "An American in Paris", to the great displeasure of patrons, who were not enamored of the chords and discords of his creative genius. Some even offered to pay for a piano tuner when they heard Gershwin working on this composition, which he noted down on paper napkins. Unfortunately those priceless napkins were used during the war to light the stove.

Although the décor helped to make Harry's Bar an (almost) all-American institution, it was the unique nature of Harry MacElhone that explained its instant success. The atmosphere and the cocktails served were all stamped with his sociable, jovial character. Harry never stopped looking for ways to entertain and amuse his patrons.

As a marketing man before the term was invented, Harry was ready to seize any opportunity to get his establishment in the news. Of course, he kept an eye on the bottom line, but above all, he wanted his bar to be a place for relaxed human interaction. He was always on hand to welcome his customers. He was a good talker and a good listener. He could sense people's moods, and they became friends even before they became customers. He always sat in the same place, just to the left of the bar entrance, ready to greet anyone who stepped inside. His friendly face and general bonhomie are inseparably linked to the image of the place. Everyone who knew him remembers him as a small, rotund man, with cropped hair, revealing a high forehead and bushy black eyebrows.

Harry MacElhone died of a heart attack on 3 June 1958. In accordance with his wishes, the bar did not close. The man who had devoted his entire life to bringing joy into other people's lives had not wanted a death announcement to be sent out, but all the barmen of Paris came to bid farewell to "Old Harry". That day, Andrew MacElhone quit his spot behind the bar to take his seat on his father's chair, facing the bar. He took over from the man who, "Scotsman by birth, American by mistaken identity, bar-tender by dedication"[2], "was known from Paris to San Francisco and from London to Singapore"[3]. "The United States has lost its most famous ambassador to Paris."[4] Andrew himself added that "For years, we told customers that he was in the back room and would be back soon…" And he is still very much present as the spirit of the place.

2. *Daily Mail*, 5 June 1958.
3. *Evening News*, 4 June 1958.
4. *Le Journal du Dimanche*, 8 June 1958.

1. Man o'War, eines der erfolgreichsten Vollblut-Rennpferde aller Zeiten / *Man o'War, one of the greatest Thoroughbred racehorses of all time*
2. Eine Postkarte, die Primo Carnera und Sparrow Robertson zeigt / *Postcard showing Primo Carnera and Sparrow*
3. Seite 36 *Die Presse-Bande* von Pandl, 1929 / The Press Gang *by Pandl, 1929.*
Le Gang de la presse, par Pandl, 1929.

WHO GOES TO HARRY'S BAR?

WER GEHT IN HARRY'S BAR ?

Als Tod Sloan die New York Bar 1911 eröffnete, wurde sie sofort zum bevorzugten Treffpunkt für sämliche Fans des Pferderennsports. Sie zog amerikanische Gäste an, die auf Dampfschiffen über den Atlantik kamen, in London einen Rolls Royce kauften und damit so lange durch Europa reisten, bis er liegenblieb. Das konnte drei Monate oder fünf Jahre dauern. Diese Gäste hielten der Bar auch die Treue, nachdem Milton und Nell Henry sie übernommen hatten. Im Krieg wurden die Pferderennen eingestellt, und die neuen Barbesitzer kehrten zurück nach Amerika. Zu den Gästen der New York Bar zählten nun auch Soldaten aller Nationalitäten, wobei Kilttragende Schotten, Australier und britische Piloten des Royal Flying Corps (RFC) deutlich überwogen. Es kamen aber auch amerikanische Freiwillige, zum Beispiel die Piloten der gefeierten Lafayette Escadrille. Diese legendären Kämpfer machten die Bar zu ihrem Hauptquartier, und diese verdankt ihnen im Gegenzug einen Teil ihres Ruhms. Als die amerikanischen Soldaten nach Kriegsende heimkehrten, hatten sie die fröhlichen Stunden nicht vergessen, und sie erzählten jedem Landsmann, dass zu einer Reise nach Paris unbedingt ein Abend in der New York Bar gehöre. Auch amerikanische Armeeangehörige, die ihren Familien zeigen wollten, wo in Frankreich sie gekämpft hatten, pilgerten in die Bar zurück, um sich zu vergewissern, dass dort noch alles beim Alten war.

Die Klientel der Bar wurde heterogener, nachdem Harry MacElhone die Leitung übernommen hatte. Auch er war ein Anhänger des Pferderennsports, doch seine wahre Leidenschaft galt dem Boxen. Und so mischten sich in der Bar die Stammbesucher der Rennbahnen in Auteuil und Longchamp mit berühmten Gesichtern des Boxsports, die man aus der Trainingshalle oder von Wettkämpfen her kannte. Jack Dempsey, Marcel Cerdan und Georges Carpentier, die alle Stammgäste bei Harry waren, lockten ihrerseits Fans in die Bar. Zu ihnen gehörte auch Ernest Hemingway. Er war mit Harry eng befreundet, und dieser verließ oft seinen Platz an der Bar, um Hemingway bei seinen Boxkämpfen auf dem Montmatre als Sekundant zur Seite zu stehen. Harry verehrte Hemingway und ließ seinen Namen auf eine Metalltafel gravieren, die er auf den Lieblings-Barhocker des Schriftstellers schraubte.

Fanden Boxkämpfe statt, bewahrte Harry zwar gern die Wetteinsätze auf die Boxer in seiner Kasse auf, nahm aber selbst nie Wetten an. Er hielt auch immer

1.

2.

When Tod Sloan opened the New York Bar in 1911, it immediately became the headquarters for all horseracing buffs. It attracted American customers who arrived by ocean liner, purchased a Rolls-Royce in London and travelled around Europe until the Rolls broke down (which could take anywhere from three months to five years). These customers remained loyal after Milton and Nell Henry had taken over the Bar, but in wartime, the horse races disappeared and with them the Bar's owners, who sailed back to the United States. By then, the New York Bar had extended its welcome to soldiers of all nationalities, with a visible majority of kilted Scots, Australians, British aviators from the Royal Flying Corps (RFC) and the first American volunteers, like the members of the celebrated Lafayette Squadron. These legendary fighter aces made the Bar their HQ, and it is to them that it owes some of its fame. After the war was over and they went home, they remembered the good times and ensured that the New York Bar was a must-see stop for any American turning up in Paris. The Doughboys who returned to France with their families to show them where they had fought, also made pilgrimages back to the Bar, to make sure that nothing had changed.

The Bar's clientele became more diversified after Harry MacElhone, a devotee of the racetrack, but with a marked preference for the world of boxing, took charge. From then on, the regulars at the Auteuil and Longchamp racetracks could be seen rubbing shoulders with familiar faces from boxing gyms and matches. Jack Dempsey, Marcel Cerdan and Georges Carpentier, regulars at Harry's, attracted their supporters. Ernest Hemingway was among them. He was great friends with Harry, who would often relinquish his seat at the bar to serve as Hemingway's second at the boxing matches he fought in Montmartre. Harry, who admired the famous barfly, had a metal plaque engraved with Hemingway's name and screwed it onto the writer's favorite bar stool.

Harry used to keep the bets placed on the boxers in the till, but never took bets himself. He also held a few seats in reserve so that latecomers still had a chance to watch bouts. It was probably that sporting atmosphere that explains the presence of so many sports commentators, because Harry's Bar was

3.

ein paar Plätze für Nachzügler frei, damit sie die Rundfunkübertragung der Kämpfe nicht verpassten. Da auch viele Sportkommentatoren in Harry's Bar auftauchten, wurde diese bald zum Sportler-Treff schlechthin. 1948 stellte Harry sogar sein eigenes Softball-Team zusammen, die Coca-Cola Kids. Sie gewannen jedes Jahr bis 1952, und dann wieder 1957 und 1959. Auch Rugby hat einen besonderen Platz in Harry's Bar. Egal woher die Teams stammten, am Ende eines Wettkampfs in Paris landeten alle bei Harry. Alle saßen dort einträchtig zusammen, Aktive und Fans, Sieger und Verlierer. Man feierte einfach gern an einem authentischen Ort gemeinsam mit anderen Sportbegeisterten.

Auch amerikanische Journalisten, die nach Frankreich geschickt worden waren, machten Harry's Bar zu ihrem Hauptquartier. Zwischen den Weltkriegen war die US-Presse in Paris stark vertreten. Auf beiden Seiten der Avenue de l'Opéra florierten die Nachrichtenagenturen. Von 43 Zeitungen, Magazinen und Agenturen, die bei der amerikanischen Handelskammer in Paris registriert waren, waren 18 nicht einmal einen Steinwurf von Harry's Bar entfernt. So verbrachten zahlreiche Reporter, vor allem der Regenbogenpresse, einen Großteil ihrer Arbeitszeit nicht im Büro, sondern in der Bar, ständig auf der Jagd nach amerikanischen Prominenten. Auch für Interviews war sie ein beliebter Treffpunkt. Einige Journalisten saßen den ganzen Tag bei Harry und schrieben ihre Artikel anhand von Informationen, die sie dort zusammengetragen hatten.

Der bekannteste unter ihnen war William »Sparrow« Robertson, der für die Pariser Ausgabe der *Herald Tribune* arbeitete. Er machte Harry's Bar bereits 1925 zu »seinem bevorzugten Durst-Tempel«. In seiner Sportkolumne »Sporting Gossip« erschien Harry's Bar oft als Schauplatz oder als Ausgangspunkt für eine Story. Häufig fand auch Harry selbst darin Erwähnung oder wurden seine Witze zitiert. Robertsons Kollegen Red Smith, Basil Woon, Hank Wales, Eric Hawkins, Vincent Sheean und O.O. MacIntyre waren ebenfalls Stammgäste in Harry's Bar.

unquestionably the sportsmen's hang-out. So much so, in fact, that Harry put together his own softball team, the *Coca-Cola Kids*, in 1948. It was victorious every year until 1952, and then again in 1957 and 1959, when the team retired. Rugby also has a special place at Harry's. The teams, regardless of their origin, ended up there after every Paris tournament. The supporters made it their base camp. Everybody met at the bar, winners and losers alike, just happy to be celebrating together in an authentic venue where the enthusiasm for sport was shared.

American journalists sent to France made Harry's Bar their headquarters, too. Between the wars, the US press kept large staffs in Paris. News agencies flourished on both sides of the Avenue de l'Opéra. Out of forty-three newspapers, magazines and news agencies identified by the American Chamber of Commerce in Paris, eighteen were located a stone's throw from Harry's Bar. It comes as no surprise to learn that it was visited by many of the reporters, who spent most of their time away from their offices tracking US celebrities. They would often set up appointments at Harry's Bar for their interviews. Nor was it unusual for some journalists to spend the whole day at Harry's, writing their articles on the basis of the information they had gleaned there.

The best-known of those journalists, William "Sparrow" Robertson, of the Paris edition of the *Herald Tribune*, made Harry's Bar "his favorite thirst emporium" as early as 1925. His Sporting Gossip column often cited Harry's as the scene of an event or the starting point for a story. He often mentioned Harry himself, who was a friend, and his jokes. Sparrow Robertson's colleagues, Red Smith, Basil Woon, Hank Wales, Eric Hawkins, Vincent Sheean and O. O. MacIntyre, were also regular patrons of Harry's Bar.

Aus dem Gästebuch: Jack Dempsey und Georges Carpentier unterschrieben dort ebenso wie Ernest Hemingway – als Boxer. Auch andere Sportler signierten diese Doppelseite, darunter Victor »Young« Perez (Boxer), Jack Root (Boxer), Charlie Santen (Boxer), Freddie Miller (Boxer), Ed »Don« George (Ringer), Bruce Barnes (Tennisspieler), Albert Burke (Tennisspieler), Jack Crawford (Tennisspieler), Suzanne Lenglen (Tennisspielerin), Charley Paddock (Sprinter). Ihre Namen stehen mitten unter anderen, die weniger mit Sport zu tun haben. Die bekanntesten sind O.O. MacIntyre, Roy Barton und Marlene Dietrich.

Jack Dempsey and Georges Carpentier signed the bar's visitors' book. Ernest Hemingway also signed it... as a boxer. Other sportsmen also signed this double page, including Victor "Young" Perez (boxer), Jack Root (boxer), Charlie Santen (boxer), Freddie Miller (boxer), Ed "Don" George (wrestler), Bruce Barnes (tennis), Albert Burke (tennis), Jack Crawford (tennis), Suzanne Lenglen (tennis), Charley Paddock (sprinter). Their names are surrounded by those of a less athletic bent, notably those of O. O. MacIntyre, Roy Barton and Marlene Dietrich. But many other names lurk on these pages...

HOME **AWAY** FROM **HOME**

ZWEITE **HEIMAT** IN **PARIS**

Außer den Prominenten, die Journalisten zum Interview in die Bar einluden, besuchten auch viele andere Gäste aus Übersee oft diesen Pariser Treffpunkt. So stieß man dort auf zahlreiche amerikanische Schriftsteller der sogenannten »Lost Generation«, die nach Frankreich ins Exil gegangen waren, um ihrer Intuition freien Lauf zu lassen. Literatur und Whisky haben sich schon immer gut vertragen, und so wurde Harry's Bar zur Stammkneipe der in Paris lebenden Autoren. So bemerkte die *Houston Post* im Mai 1974: »Harry's Liste an Stammgästen, damals wie heute, liest sich wie ein Who is Who der Literatur.« Einer der treuesten Stammgäste war Ernest Hemingway, der 1919 zum ersten Mal durch die Schwingtüren trat. Damals war er nur einer von vielen jungen Reportern, die aus dem Krieg zurückkehrten. Oft sah man ihn in Gesellschaft von F. Scott Fitzgerald und dessen Frau Zelda. Weitere Gäste waren William Saroyan, Sinclair Lewis, Thornton Wilder, John Dos Passos und John Steinbeck. Sie erschienen häufig in Begleitung von Hollywoodstars, wie Douglas Fairbanks, dem großen Stummfilmstar der Zwanzigerjahre, Gene Kelly und Buster Keaton. Unter den Sportlern, die regelmäßig die Bar besuchten, waren Primo Carnera, Jack Dempsey, Young Perez, Jack Root, Charlie Santen (alias Wally Dusek) und Freddie Miller (alle Boxer), die Tennisspieler Jack Crawford und Albert Burke, der Rennfahrer Barney Oldfield und der Jockey Earl Sande. Auch an musikalischer Prominenz mangelte es nicht. Der Meistgesehene war George Gershwin, aber auch Cole Porter und Rudolf Friml kamen oft vorbei. Und im Glanz der Stars sonnten sich die Politiker jener Zeit, wie James Walker, der Bürgermeister von New York City von 1925 bis 1932, und Franklin Delano Roosevelt Jr., der Sohn des amerikanischen Präsidenten. Weitere Besucher waren der Prince of Wales, der nachmalige König Edward VIII. und George O. Noville, der Harry ein Telegramm aus der Antarktis schickte: »Viel Eis hier, aber die restlichen Zutaten fehlen!«

Ein paar Barhocker gab es auch für Nichtamerikaner, häufig besetzt von den Drehbuchautoren Jacques Prévert und Marcel Achard, den Boxern Marcel Cerdan und Georges Carpentier und dem Tennisstar Suzanne Lenglen.[5]

5. Suzanne Lenglen, 1899 geboren und als *Die Göttliche* betitelt. Sie war der erste weibliche Tennisstar in Frankreich nach dem Ersten Weltkrieg.

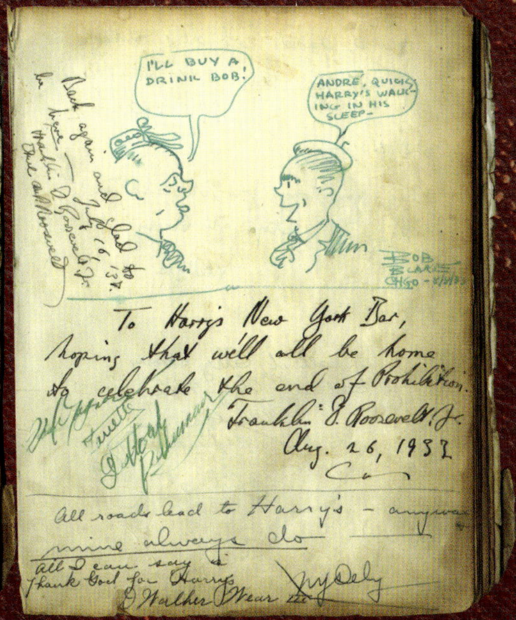

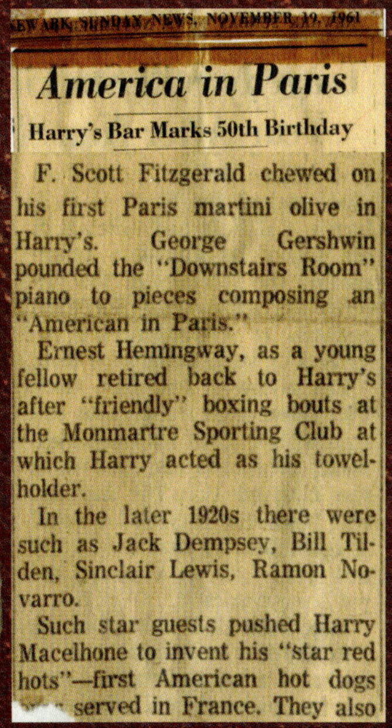

NEWARK SUNDAY NEWS, NOVEMBER 19, 1961

America in Paris

Harry's Bar Marks 50th Birthday

F. Scott Fitzgerald chewed on his first Paris martini olive in Harry's. George Gershwin pounded the "Downstairs Room" piano to pieces composing an "American in Paris."

Ernest Hemingway, as a young fellow retired back to Harry's after "friendly" boxing bouts at the Monmartre Sporting Club at which Harry acted as his towel-holder.

In the later 1920s there were such as Jack Dempsey, Bill Tilden, Sinclair Lewis, Ramon Novarro.

Such star guests pushed Harry Macelhone to invent his "star red hots"—first American hot dogs ... served in France. They also

In addition to the celebrities the journalists brought to the Bar to interview, there were many others who frequented the Paris meeting point. Large numbers of US writers of the "Lost Generation" who had exiled themselves to France to give their imaginations free rein could be seen there. Because writing and whisky have always gone well together, Harry's Bar was the watering hole for the authors of Paris ("A list of Harry's regular patrons, past and present, reads like a *Who's Who* of literature," *Houston Post*, May 1974). One of its stalwarts was none other than Ernest Hemingway, who pushed through the batwings for the very first time in 1919. At that point, he was just another young reporter back from the war. He was often seen in the company of F. Scott Fitzgerald and his wife, Zelda. Also stopping by were William Saroyan, Sinclair Lewis, Thornton Wilder, John Dos Passos and John Steinbeck. They were often accompanied by the Hollywood stars of the day, including Douglas Fairbanks, the great silent movie actor in the 1920s, Gene Kelly and Buster Keaton. The sportsmen included Primo Carnera, Jack Dempsey, Young Perez, Jack Root, Charlie Santen (aka Wally Dusek) and Freddie Miller (all US boxers), tennis players Jack Crawford and Albert Burke, racing driver Barney Oldfield and jockey Earl Sande. Nor was there any lack of musicians, with George Gershwin leading the charge, followed by Cole Porter and Rudolf Friml. Not to be left out were leading politicians like James Walker, the mayor of New York from 1925 to 1932, and Franklin Delano Roosevelt Jr. (the son of the president). Other visitors included the Prince of Wales (the future King Edward VIII) and Lieutenant Commander George O. Noville, who sent a telegram to Harry during his expedition to the South Pole: "Plenty ice here but other ingredients missing!"

There were still a few bar stools free for non-Americans, and French celebrities also haunted Harry's Bar, including screenwriters Jacques Prévert and Marcel Achard, boxers Marcel Cerdan and Georges Carpentier and tennis star Suzanne Lenglen[5].

5. Born in 1899, and nicknamed *La Divine*, she was the first French female tennis star before and after WWI.

1. **Seite 44** Jess Hahn, ein amerikanischer Schauspieler, der in Frankreich lebt, gibt bei der Straw Vote (Testabstimmung) 1964 (Lyndon B. Johnson vs. Barry Goldwater) seine Stimme ab. / *Jess Hahn, an American actor living in France, votes during the Straw vote of 1964 (Lyndon B. Johnson vs Barry Goldwater)*
2. **Seite 48** Mitten in der Prohibition importiert Harry aus den USA ganze Fässer »Prohibitionsbier«. / *At the height of the Prohibition era in the US, Harry imported whole barrels of "Prohibition Beer".*

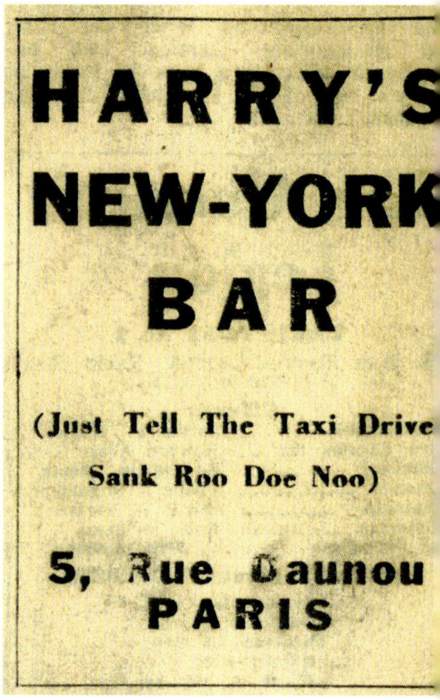

SANK ROO DOE **NOO**

5 RUE DAUNOU

Der kometenhafte Erfolg der Bar ist zum Großteil auf Harry selbst zurückzuführen. Er war stets darum bemüht, dass seine Gäste sich bei ihm zu Hause fühlten, und landete eine Reihe von Marketing-Coups. Zunächst startete er eine umfangreiche Werbekampagne und brachte Stunden damit zu, Freunden in aller Welt seine neue Adresse mitzuteilen und sie auf einen Besuch einzuladen. 1924 gab er eine Anzeige in der Pariser Ausgabe der *New York Herald Tribune* auf:

SAGEN SIE DEM TAXIFAHRER EINFACH
SANK ROO DOE NOO
UND MACHEN SIE SICH AUF DAS SCHLIMMSTE GEFASST

»Sank Roo Doe Noo«: Diese seltsame Zauberformel, die Journalisten wegen Harrys schottischer Herkunft lange für Gälisch hielten, war nichts anderes als die Adresse der Bar in Lautschrift: 5 Rue Danou. Auf diese Weise wollte Harry erreichen, dass jeder Englischsprechende, der nach Paris kam, von den Taxifahrern gleich zu seiner Bar gebracht wurde. Der Slogan wird auch heute noch benutzt und taucht regelmäßig auf den Seiten der *International Herald Tribune* auf. Harrys genialer Einfall wurde ein Erfolg. Amerikanische Touristen rannten ihm die Tür ein. Junge Männer kamen vorbei, um ihm Grüße von ihren Vätern und manchmal sogar ihren Großvätern auszurichten. Einige kannten Harry noch von der Zeit, als Tod Sloan die Bar gehörte und Harry nur Barkeeper war, oder von seiner Zeit in London. Auch damals schon mochten ihn die Leute wegen seines Frohsinns und seiner Warmherzigkeit.

»Straw **Vote**«

1924 veranstaltete Harry die erste Straw Vote: eine Wahl »zum Spaß«, an der alle Amerikaner über 21 (seit 1971 über 18), die in Paris lebten oder sich dort während der Präsidentschaftswahl aufhielten, teilnehmen konnten. Damals gab es noch keine Briefwahl, daher hatten solche Testabstimmungen für Auslandsamerikaner eine besondere Bedeutung. 1924 wurde John Calvin Coolidge Jr. zum 30. Präsidenten der Vereinigten Staaten gewählt, erst in Harry's Bar und dann in ganz Amerika.

Die Kampagne begann einen Monat vor dem Wahltag in den USA. Jeden Tag kamen Amerikaner vorbei und steckten ihren Wahlzettel in die vorbereitete Urne. Die Stimmen wurden jedes Wochenende ausgezählt und die Ergebnisse in weißer Farbe auf dem großen Spiegel hinter der Bar bekanntgegeben. Das Verfahren wurde sehr ernst genommen. Es war nicht erlaubt, zweimal zu wählen oder die Ergebnisse zu

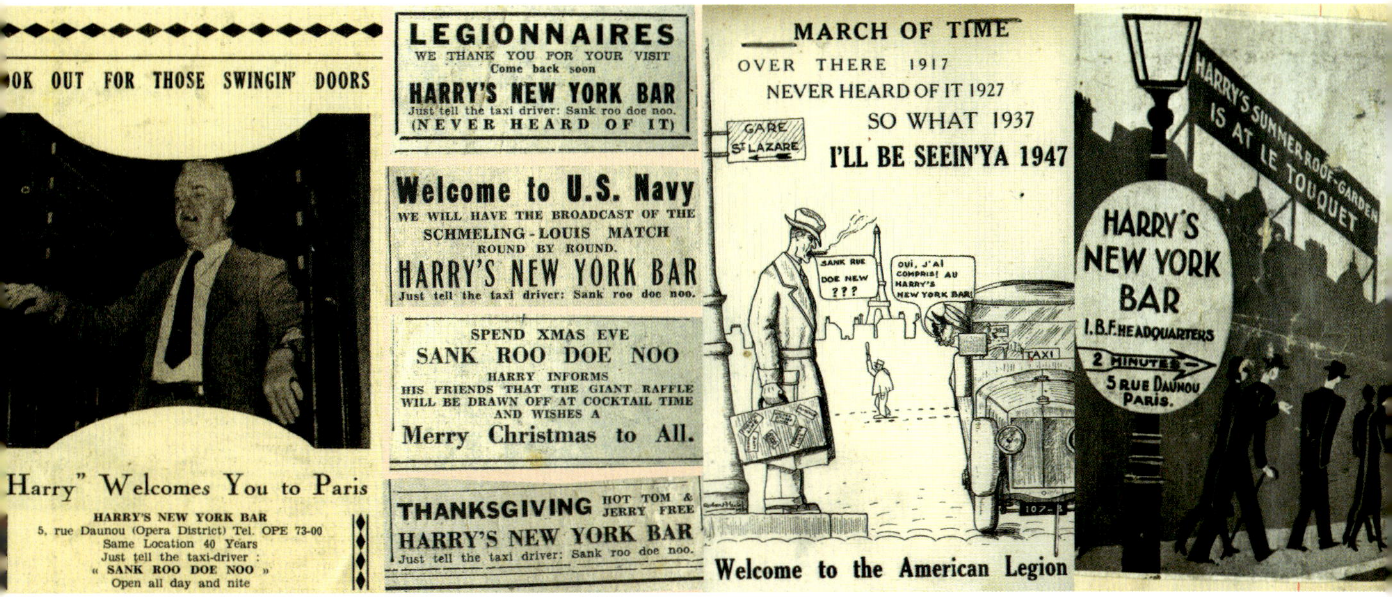

Much of the Bar's meteoric success can be put down to Harry himself. He did everything he could to make people feel at home and brought off a succession of marketing coups. Initially, he embarked on a full-scale advertising campaign, and spent long hours writing personally to all his friends all over the world, giving them his new address and inviting them to visit. In 1924, he placed an ad in the Paris edition of the *New York Herald Tribune*:

JUST TELL THE TAXI DRIVER

SANK ROO DOE NOO

AND GET READY FOR THE WORST

"Sank Roo Doe Noo": the strange incantation, which journalists, remembering the owner's Scottish origins, long thought was Gaelic, was nothing other than the phonetic transcription of the Bar's address: 5, rue Daunou. It was meant to enable any English-speaking person turning up in Paris to be understood by any taxi driver and be taken to the right address, i.e., Harry's Bar, without difficulty. The slogan is still in use today, and regularly appears in the pages of the *International Herald Tribune*. Harry's brainstorm was a success. American tourists beat a track to his door. Young men dropped by to say hello to Harry from their fathers and sometimes their grandfathers. Some had known Harry when he was only a barman during Tod Sloan's tenure, or from his time in London. But even in those early days, people loved his bonhomie and general good humor.

The **Straw** Vote

In 1924, Harry organized the first **Straw vote**: an election "for fun" in which all Americans, aged 21 or over (18 or over since 1971), living or staying in Paris at the time of each US presidential election, were invited to take part. Absentee voting did not exist at the time, and this "Straw vote" took on a special significance for Americans in Paris. In 1924, John Calvin Coolidge Jr. was elected 30th President of the United States at Harry's – and in the United States.

The campaign begins a month before Election Day in the United States. Each day, Americans stop by to drop their ballot in the urn specially designed for the event. The ballots are counted every weekend, and the results posted in white paint on the large mirror behind the bar.

1.

manipulieren. Die Wähler mussten ihre Stimmzettel unterschreiben und ihre Identität nachweisen.

24 Stunden bevor Amerika seinen neuen Präsidenten verkündete, hatten die Amerikaner in Paris ihren schon bestimmt. Bis zum Zweiten Weltkrieg – während des Krieges gab es keine Straw Vote – wurde die Wahl der Amerikaner in Paris immer durch ihre Landsleute bestätigt. 1928 schlug Herbert Hoover Al Smith mit 444 zu 87 Stimmen, und 1932 unterlag er Franklin D. Roosevelt mit 158 zu 288 Stimmen. Die Barbesucher lagen in 87 Jahren und 25 Wahlen nur zweimal daneben, was die Abstimmung in Harry's Bar zur verlässlichsten Meinungsumfrage für Präsidentschaftswahlen gemacht hat. Das erste Mal lagen sie 1976 falsch, als sie für Gerald Ford stimmten und Jimmy Carter gewählt wurde, das zweite Mal, als sie George W. Bush nicht wiederwählten. Der Grund dafür ist vermutlich im Boykott Frankreichs durch die Republikaner zu suchen. Dadurch waren sie in der Rue Daunou zweifellos unterrepräsentiert.

Am Wahlabend fand stets eine Party statt, bei der die Glücklichen, die Eingang fanden, die Bekanntgabe der Ergebnisse live im Radio mitverfolgten. Dabei platzte die Bar aus allen Nähten. Das Spektakel war beeindruckend: Man hängte Zettel mit den Namen der Bundesstaaten an einen Draht, der um die ganze Bar herumgespannt war. Wenn die Stimmen eines Bundesstaates ausgezählt waren, wurde das Ergebnis auf dem entsprechenden Zettel notiert, sofern man den Moderator durch die lauten Jubelschreie und Pfiffe hören konnte. Unabhängig vom Wahlausgang war dieser Abend immer eine gute Gelegenheit, das Ereignis an sich zu feiern. Es fehlte nicht an Trinksprüchen sowohl auf den Gewinner als auch auf den Verlierer – ein Vorwand, um noch mehr zu trinken. Die Straw Vote findet nach wie vor alle vier Jahre statt. 2008 schlug Obama McCain mit 272 zu 170 Stimmen. Es war eine tolle Party. Die Zettel wurden inzwischen durch Fernsehbilder ersetzt, aber die Rue Daunou ist an diesem Abend immer noch brechend voll. Die Straße wird sogar für den Verkehr gesperrt, während die Weltpresse in Harry's Bar strömt, um über das Ereignis zu berichten.

International **Bar Fly**

IBF (FBI rückwärts gelesen) sind die Initialen des Barvereins »International Bar Fly«, gegründet 1924 von Harry MacElhone, der jede Gelegenheit beim Schopf packte, seine Bar ins Gespräch zu bringen. Harrys Freund Oscar Odd MacIntyre, ein Reporter der *Chicago Evening Post*, hatte ihn eines Tages auf die Idee gebracht, als er seine tägliche Kolumne *Paris, Day by Day* abschloss. Der Name entstammt einer Kolumne, in der MacIntyre beschrieb, wie am Vorabend eine Gruppe amerikanischer Journalisten, darunter Basil Woon, Korrespondent von *Universal Service Inc.*, Carl Dennewitz, der für die Pari-

The American WEEKEND

The Family Newspaper For Americans Overseas

6 No. 8 – 20 Cents July 4, 1959

Harry's Bar is famous as well for being the home of the I.B.F. (International Bar Flies), an organization founded by Hemingway, with Cole Porter, Sinclair Lewis, Gershwin, Jack Dempsey and Carpentier as charter members.

Each member of the club is equipped with a booklet giving the rules and a list of other establishments around the world where he will find friendly bottle flies.

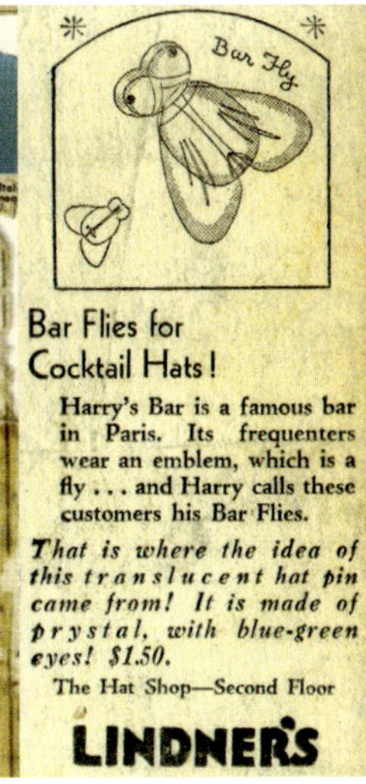

The procedure is taken very seriously. It is unacceptable to vote twice or to falsify the results. Voters are asked to sign their ballots and to show proof of identity. Twenty-four hours before the United States reveals the name of the new president, the Americans in Paris have designated theirs. Until WWII (no "Straw votes" were held during the war), the choice of the Americans in Paris was always ratified by those at home. In 1928, Herbert Hoover defeated Al Smith in Paris by 444 votes to 87, and in 1932, Hoover was beaten by Franklin Roosevelt by 288 votes to 158. Harry's Bar's patrons have only been wrong on two occasions in 87 years and 25 elections, making it one of the world's most reliable opinion pollsters. The first wrong call came in 1976 when Harry's Bar voted for Gerald Ford, but Jimmy Carter was elected, and the second was when the Bar's American patrons failed to re-elect George W. Bush. The explanation probably lies in the boycott of France, and hence of Paris, by the Republicans: their representation in Rue Daunou no doubt suffered.

Generally, a party is held in the evening of Election Day, when the lucky ones able to get inside would listen to the live radio transmission of the official results. During the party, Harry's Bar would be bursting at the seams. The spectacle inside was impressive: sheets of paper were hung on a wire running right round the bar, each with the name of a US State written on it. The outcome of the voting was tracked on these as the results came in, if the commentator's voice could be heard above the din of cheers and catcalls. Whoever the winner, the evening is always an opportunity to celebrate the event, and numerous toasts are made to the winner (and to the loser, too, as an excuse to have another drink). The "Straw vote" is still organized every four years, and in 2008, Obama beat McCain 272 to 170. It was a great party. The sheets of paper have now been replaced by the screens of the news agencies and TV channels, but Rue Daunou still rocks with people. It is even closed to traffic on that evening, while the world's media flock to Harry's to record the event.

International **Bar Fly**

I.B.F. (which reads F.B.I. the other way round) are the initials of the International Bar Fly association, set up in 1924 by Harry MacElhone, ever-ready to seize the slightest opportunity to get people talking about his Bar. Harry's friend, Oscar Odd MacIntyre, a reporter with the *Chicago Evening Post*, gave him the idea one day as he was wrapping up his copy for his daily Paris, Day by Day column. The name comes from the column in which he retraces the journey taken the evening before by a group of American journalists, when Basil Woon, correspondent of *Universal Service Inc.*, Carl Dennewitz,

ser Ausgabe der *Chicago Tribune* arbeitete, und ein Dutzend weiterer Kollegen auf »Kneipentour« ging. Sie starteten im Chatham, zogen dann in die Bar des Hotel Ritz und weiter zu Lew Hauser in der Rue Caumartin und zu Freddie Payne in der Rue Blanche, bevor sie schließlich bei Zelli am Place Pigalle landeten. Und überall nahmen sie einen Drink. Am Ende der Tour klebte Carl Dennewitz tote Fliegen auf Zuckerstücke, von denen jeder der Anwesenden sich eines ans Revers steckte. Dieses Motiv wurde später in verschiedenen Varianten auf dem Boden von Harry's Bar verewigt. MacIntyres Artikel titelte *Barflies of Paris*, und gleich am nächsten Tag wurde der Verein gegründet. Harry's Bar war dabei die Trap (Falle) Nr. 1. Binnen kurzer Zeit folgten Dutzende mehr, die über den ganzen Globus verteilt waren.[6]

Der Club bekam eine eigene Hymne, komponiert von Leo Deslys und Roy Barton, und eine humorvolle Satzung. Artikel eins ist ein gutes Beispiel: *Eine geheime und heilige Bruderschaft, die sich der Erbauung und dem Ruin schwerer Trinker verschrieben hat.* Die Gründungsmitglieder waren O. O. MacIntyre als Vorsitzender, Harry MacElhone als stellvertretender Vorsitzender, das Barpersonal und die Reporter vom Vorabend. Nach und nach öffnete sich der Verein auch einem größeren Kreis. Doch um Mitglied zu werden, musste man eine beträchtliche Menge Alkohol vertragen und von zwei Vereinsmitgliedern bei der Bewerbung unterstützt werden. Die Liste derer, die in den Zwischenkriegsjahren dem Verein beitraten, umfasst unter anderem Ernest Hemingway, Sinclair Lewis, Jack Dempsey, Floyd Gibbons, W. R. Hearst Jr., Cole Porter, Earl Sande, Douglas Fairbanks, Georges Carpentier, George Gershwin, Jack Donohue, Erskine Gwynne, General Dwight D. Eisenhower, Lieutenant Commander Noville, Franklin D. Roosevelt Jr., Wythe Williams, Preston Sturges, Thornton Wilder und Burt Lancaster. Die Liste wurde jedoch im Lauf der Jahre immer länger.

Sobald man zugelassen ist, erhält man einen Ausweis mit dem Logo des IBF – zwei sich grüßende Fliegen in Frack und Zylinder – und ein personalisiertes Büchlein, in dem die Vereinsstatuten und die dem Verein zugehörigen Bars aufgelistet sind. Beschrieben wird außerdem das Begrüßungszeremoniell, anhand dessen sich Mitglieder erkennen: *Du darfst einen Gast nicht direkt fragen: »Bist du ein Barfly?« Stattdessen gehst du mit fröhlicher Miene auf ihn zu und schwingst, wenn möglich, ein Glas in der linken Hand. Mit der rechten tu so, als wischtest du dir vorsichtig eine Fliege von der linken Schulter. Falls er auch ein IBF ist, wird er mit kecker Miene auf dich zu eilen und dasselbe Ritual vollziehen, während er gleichzeitig mit dir eine große summende Honigbiene imitiert: Bss, bss, bss ... Dann hebt ein jeder von euch den linken Fuß 25 Zentimeter an – was der üblichen Höhe der Fußbank in der Bar entspricht –, ihr gebt euch die rechte Hand und krümmt die Finger so, als haltet ihr darin ein volles Glas White Horse oder ein Pint Ingwerbier.*

Der IBF ist als Verein immer noch aktiv. Es gibt viele Anwärter, aber nur wenige schaffen die Aufnahme. Auch einige Frauen sind schon lange Teil des erlesenen Zirkels. Elsa Maxwell, Klatschkolumnistin und Veranstalterin mondäner Partys, und der Filmstar Michèle Morgan waren die ersten weiblichen Zugänge. Und auch in Romanen wird der IBF erwähnt, etwa in *La Chambre de ton père*[7]; darin verweist Michel Déon auf die »silbernen Manschettenknöpfe mit den eingravierten Buchstaben IBF, dem Geheimzeichen des International Bar Fly«.

Home, Sweet Home

Harry's Bar ist echt amerikanisch. Seit 1919 wird dort auch **Coca Cola** angeboten. Es war die erste Bar in Frankreich, die die legendäre amerikanische Brause führte. Man kann dort außerdem jeden Tag **amerikanische Zeitungen** lesen, und die offizielle Verkehrssprache ist Englisch. Einige Kellner sind Amerikaner, was es für Touristen aus Amerika leichter macht, nach dem Weg zu Sehenswürdigkeiten zu fragen. Am Ende ziehen sie einem Museumsbesuch meist den Genuss eines Getränks vor. Harry selbst war schon bald mehr Amerikaner als Schotte. Viele seiner Gäste wussten nicht einmal, woher er stammte. Bereits im Jahr 1926 führte die amerikanische Handelskammer in Frankreich Harry als amerikanischen Einwohner.

1933 kaufte Harry schließlich auf der Weltausstellung in Chicago zur endgültigen »Amerikanisierung« seiner Bar eine Hot-Dog-Maschine. Die ersten **Hot Dogs** von ganz Frankreich wurden also in seiner Bar angeboten. Man spülte sie üblicherweise mit ein, zwei Bier hinunter.

6. Manche haben versucht, einen Teil dieses Ausdrucks, der heute auf der ganzen Welt gebräuchlich ist, kommerziell zu nutzen, wodurch der Eigentümer dieser eingetragenen Marke sich gezwungen sah, ihn von allen gewerblichen Schildern entfernen zu lassen. Harry's Bar schläft nie ...!
7. Gallimard, 2004, S. 81.

of the Paris edition of the *Chicago Tribune*, and a dozen other journalists left Harry's to "tour the bars". They began at the Chatham, moved on to the bar at the Hotel Ritz, and then to Lew Hauser's, Rue Caumartin, Freddie Payne's, Rue Blanche, and ended up at Zelli's on Place Pigalle. They had a few drinks in each establishment and, before leaving, Carl Dennewitz stuck dead flies onto lumps of sugar and everyone present wore this insignia on their jacket lapel – a motif that was later reproduced with variations on the floor in Harry's Bar. MacIntyre's article was entitled "Barflies of Paris". The organization was founded the very next day. Harry's Bar was Trap No.1. Within a short time, there were several dozen others in every part of the globe[6].

An anthem in honor of the fraternity was composed by Leo Deslys and Roy Barton, and a humorous charter was penned. Article One is a good example: "A secret and sacred fraternal organization devoted to the uplift and downfall of serious drinkers." The founding members were O. O. MacIntyre, president; Harry MacElhone, vice president; the bar staff and the reporters of the evening before. Subsequently, the organization was opened to the wider public. But to become a member, you had to be able to imbibe a serious amount of alcohol and be sponsored by two existing members. The honor roll of people admitted by their choice or voted in by others between the wars includes Ernest Hemingway, Sinclair Lewis, Jack Dempsey, Floyd Gibbons, W. R. Hearst Jr., Cole Porter, Earl Sande, Douglas Fairbanks, Georges Carpentier, George Gershwin, Jack Donohue, Erskine Gwynne, General Dwight D. Eisenhower, Lieutenant Commander Noville, Franklin D. Roosevelt Jr., Wythe Williams, Preston Sturges, Thornton Wilder and Burt Lancaster. The list got longer as the years went by.

Once initiated, candidates receive a badge with the emblem of the I.B.F. (two flies in top hat and tails greeting each other) and a booklet with their name on it containing the rules to be observed and a list of member establishments. It also contains a description of the greeting used by members to recognize each other: "You must not ask a patron 'Are you a barfly?', but you must walk towards him, with a jovial air, and, if possible, brandishing a glass in your left hand. With your right hand, delicately make as if to brush an imaginary fly off your left shoulder. At that precise moment, if he too is an I.B.F., he is required to rush at you, with ribald air, to perform the same ritual, simultaneously imitating, as well as you would do yourself, the buzzing of a large honey bee: bzz, bzz, bzz, bzz... Then, each raising the left foot nine inches off the ground (the usual height of the bar's footrest), you will shake hands with the right hand, your fingers bent as if holding a full tumbler of White Horse or a pint of ginger beer."

The I.B.F. is still an active organization to this day. There are many hopefuls, but few are chosen. In his novel *La Chambre de ton père*[7], Michel Déon refers to the "silver cufflinks engraved with the letters I.B.F., the secret sign of the International Bar Fly." Women have long been admitted into the select circle. Gossip columnist and professional hostess Elsa Maxwell and film star Michèle Morgan were the first female inductees.

Home, Sweet Home

Harry's Bar is a real American bar: they've been serving **Coca-Cola** here since 1919 (it was the first bar in France to offer the legendary American tipple). You can also read **American newspapers** every day, and English is its "official" language. Some of the waiters are American, a relief for US tourists asking for directions: they generally decide to stay and have a drink rather than heading for the museums. Harry was soon more American than Scots. In fact, many of his customers had no idea about his original nationality. As early as 1926, the American Chamber of Commerce in France listed Harry as an American resident!

In 1933, to complete the "Americanization" of his bar, Harry purchased a **hot dog** machine at the Chicago World's Fair. So the first ever hot dogs to be served in France were to be found at Harry's Bar. They were generally washed down with one or more beers.

6. There are those who have tried to exploit part of this expression, today a household word around the globe, forcing the owner of the registered trademark to have it removed from all commercial signs alluding to it. Harry's Bar never sleeps... !

7. Gallimard, Paris, 2004, p. 81.

2.

Harry rief auch den **Biertrink-Wettbewerb** ins Leben. Ziel war es, zwei Liter Bier in möglichst kurzer Zeiteit hinunterzuschütten. Der amtierende Meister, ein ehemaliger Princeton-Absolvent namens Henry Cochran, erfüllte die Aufgabe am 26. Juni 1932 in elf Sekunden. Marcel Achard, der danebenstand und die Zeit nahm, staunte nicht schlecht. Cochran wurde für diese Leistung mit einem Eintrag in das Guiness Buch der Rekorde belohnt.

Seinem Ruf getreu, schenkte Harry auch sogenanntes **Prohibitionsbier** aus, das aus Amerika geliefert wurde, ein Gebräu auf Pflanzenbasis, das sich wesentlich von dem originalen Getränk unterschied. Und 1933 zur Feier der Ratifizierung des 21. Zusatzartikels zur Verfassung der Vereinigten Staaten, mit dem die Prohibition wieder abgeschafft wurde, importierte er mehrere Fässer des jetzt legalen Biers – zur Überraschung und großen Begeisterung der ganzen amerikanischen Gemeinde in Paris, die diese Geste als Sympathiebekundung der Bar verstand und als Bekräftigung, dass eine unschöne Periode in der Geschichte ihres Landes zu Ende ging. Der Tag wurde umso denkwürdiger, als das Bier nicht nur reichlich floss, sondern obendrein umsonst war.

Amerikanern, die auf der Durchreise waren, bot Harry's Bar die Möglichkeit, ihre Adresse zu hinterlassen. Harry hatte ein Buch drucken lassen mit dem Titel *Let Your Friends Know Where You Are Here* (Gib deinen Freunden Bescheid, wo du hier abgestiegen bist), in das jeder Gast den Namen des Hotels, in dem er wohnte, und die Dauer seines Aufenthalts eintragen konnte. Das Buch gibt es immer noch, und jeder kann es einsehen. So kann man mit Freunden in Kontakt treten, von deren Parisaufenthalt man nichts wusste. Längst ist Harry's Bar ein Ort, an dem soziale Netzwerke gepflegt werden. Denn es war seine lobenswerte Absicht, die internationale Verständigung und Zusammenarbeit durch ein, zwei Drinks zu erleichtern. Dafür waren auch die Streichholzbriefchen gedacht, auf deren Innenklappe in den Hauptsprachen der Welt »Zum Wohl« stand und die Harry ab 1949 an seine Gäste verteilte.

1929 nach dem Börsencrash wurden in Harry's Bar Papierservietten mit der Aufschrift **Crying Towels** (Tränentücher) verteilt, um die Gäste zu trösten und der dramatischen Lage den Ernst zu nehmen. Als deutsche Truppen 1939 in der Tschechoslowakei einmarschierten, verteilte Harry Ohrenstöpsel, um die Latrinenparolen nicht hören zu müssen.

Harry also created the "**Beer Drinking contest**". The aim is to down a two-quart glass of beer in record time. The reigning champion is a Princeton alumnus, one Henry Cochran, who on 26 June 1932, downed his two quarts in eleven seconds in the presence of an amazed Marcel Achard, tasked with timing the challenge. His reward was to feature in the *Guinness Book of World Records*.

True to its reputation, Harry's also had several cases of "**Prohibition Beer**" shipped over from the US. This was a plant-based tipple, considerably different from the original beverage. In 1933, to celebrate the ratification of Amendment XXI abolishing Prohibition, he imported several barrels of the newly legal beer. This was a great surprise and a source of immense joy to the entire American community in Paris, who saw the gesture as the expression of the friendly feelings of the bar and the end of an unhappy period in their country's history. That day was made all the more memorable by the fact that the beer flowed in abundance and was free!

When Americans were simply passing through Paris, Harry's offered them the possibility of leaving their addresses. He had a book printed entitled ***Let Your Friends Know You Are Here***, where anyone can enter the name of the hotel where he was staying and the dates he would be there. The book can be consulted freely at the bar, enabling people to get in touch with people they didn't know were coming to Paris. Social networks have been around for many years at Harry's Bar! Harry's praiseworthy intention was to facilitate international understanding and cooperation over a drink or two, like the match-books given free to customers from 1949 on, with the word "Cheers" inside the flap, translated into the world's main languages.

In 1929, after the stock market crash, Harry's Bar gave its patrons paper napkins printed with the words **Crying Towels** to comfort them, making light of a dramatic situation. In 1939, when German forces occupied Czechoslovakia and rumors of impending war were flying about, Harry handed out **Ear Plugs** to block out the pessimistic rumors.

HARRY'S BAR
5, RUE DAUNOU (OPERA) PARIS
Cocktails 6frs., Baby Whisky 6frs., Bass on Tap 3frs., Snacks all hours
"Front Page" Cabaret downstairs 10 p.m. Marie Janyl and Roy Barton entertain.

AFTER THE DAVIS CUP — COME TO
HARRY'S
"FRONT PAGE" CABARET
From 10 o'clock onwards.
5, RUE DANNOU
(Opéra)

"THE SCOTCH HOOSE"
HARRY'S BAR
5, RUE DAUNOU — PARIS

HARRY'S BAR
SAY TO DRIVER
SANK ROO
DOE NOO
and
EXPECT THE
WORST
If Walking
5, rue
Daunou
Opera Dist.
Bar open all
day and night

KEEP
COOL
Visit the
Front
Page
Cabaret
Harry's
New
York
Bar
5, rue
Daunou
Opera Dist.
Bar open all
day and night

I'LL BE SEEIN' YA
COCKTAIL TIME
HARRY'S
NEW YORK BAR
5 Rue Daunou — PARIS
(Opéra District)
Cabaret Every Evening at 10
LADIES' SALON DOWNSTAIRS

MODEL AIRCRAFT KITS
THE MODEL AIRCRAFT STORES,
133, Richmond Park Rd., Bournemouth.
For all Materials, Blueprints, Kits, Rubber, Propellers, etc. Please send 1½d. stamp for lists.

Bars
HARRY'S (ex-R.A.F.). Bass on tap. Snacks. Say to driver, "Sank Roo Doenoo," and expect the worst. Harry's New York Bar, 5 Rue Daunou 5, Paris, France.

WE DON'T IMITATE—WE INITIATE
LOOK AT THE REDUCTIONS
All Cocktails, 5fr. — All Apéritifs, 4fr.
Walsheim Beer & Bass, 3fr.
Pilsen, 4fr. — All Whiskies, 9fr.
CABARET — SAME PRICES
HARRY'S NEW YORK BAR

BOXING
SCHMELING-HAMAS FIGHT
ALL-EXPENSE TOUR
CONAGVO, 52 Av. des Champs-Elysées
Tel.: ELY. 29-63.
After 6 p.m.: HARRY'S NEW YORK BAR.

3.2 U.S. BEER
sold out except one bottle Budweiser and one bottle Pabst Blue Ribbon. The two last bottles will be sold for one thousand francs and will be given to the American Legion Poppy Fund.
HARRY'S NEW YORK BAR
5 RUE DAUNOU (Opera district).

3.2 U.S. BEER
arrives at HARRY'S NEW YORK BAR
5 RUE DAUNOU
4 O'CLOCK TUESDAY
Note: First American Beer imported since 13 yrs.

U.S. 3.2 BEER
BUDWEISER SOLD OUT — FRESH LOAD OF PABST BLUE RIBBON NOW ON SALE
HARRY'S NEW YORK BAR
5 RUE DAUNOU
A little street where all friends meet.

HARRY'S NEW YORK BAR
SAY TO DRIVER SANK ROO DOE NOO
CABARET EVERY NITE FROM 10 P.M.
LADIES STEAM ROOM
BAR OPEN ALL DAY AND NIGHT

HARRY'S NEW YORK BAR
Say to Driver: SANK ROO DOE NOO
CABARET EVERY NITE FROM 10 P.M.
LADIES' STEAM ROOM
BAR OPEN ALL DAY AND NIGHT

3.2 U.S. BEER
BUDWEISER and PABST SOLD OUT
But we have always on tap Pilsen, Walsheim, Comete, Augustinerbräu, Prinzbräu, Bass, Barley Wine.
HARRY'S NEW YORK BAR
5 RUE DAUNOU, PARIS.
FRONT PAGE CABARET EVERY NIGHT

HELLO EVERYBODY MERRY XMAS
MISS REPEAL AND MISTER VOLSTEAD HAVE ARRIVED AT HARRY'S NEW YORK BAR AND WILL BE RAFFLED OFF TONIGHT.
CABARET, FIREWORKS AND CRACKERS
SAY TO DRIVER SANK ROO DOE NOO.

HARRY'S NEW YORK BAR
Say to Driver Sank Roo Doe Noo.

SOYEZ DE L'EPOQUE !...
Allez au
HARRY'S BAR
5, rue Daunou
Cabaret tous les soirs.

L'EPOQUE
Mercredi 9 Juin 1937

BRITONS IN PARIS
Listen-in to the Coronation Ceremony
at HARRY'S BAR
5, RUE DAUNOU (Opéra district)
and try A 1937 CORONATION COCKTAIL

. . . . Good Bars . . . .
A.1 at HARRY'S. Every nite cabaret. Glover at the piano. Just tell the driver sank roo doe noo (5 Rue Daunou, Opéra).

. . . . Good Bars . . . .
AMERICAN BAR. Just tell the taxi driver: Sank Roo Doe Noo, and he will take you straight to Harry's New York Bar.

EVERYBODY WELCOME!
to listen to
the CORONATION CEREMONY at
HARRY'S NEW YORK BAR
Just tell the taxi driver: Sank roo doe noo.
and try
Our 1937 CORONATION COCKTAIL!

LEGIONNAIRES
WE THANK YOU FOR YOUR VISIT
Come back soon
HARRY'S NEW YORK BAR
Just tell the taxi driver: Sank roo doe noo.
(NEVER HEARD OF IT)

SPEND XMAS EVE
SANK ROO DOE NOO
HARRY INFORMS
HIS FRIENDS THAT THE GIANT RAFFLE
WILL BE DRAWN OFF AT COCKTAIL TIME
AND WISHES A
Merry Christmas to All.

MERRY XMAS
TO YOU
HARRY'S NEW YORK BAR
5 RUE DAUNOU
IF YOU ARE LONELY, DROP IN.
Raffle—Live Pig, Goose. — CABARET.

MERRY XMAS
TO YOU
HARRY'S NEW YORK BAR
5 Rue Daunou
GET YOUR RAFFLE TICKET NOW
LIVE PIG & GOOSE, ETC., ETC.
CABARET ALL NIGHT

WHETHER YOU LIKE IT OR NOT
HAPPY NEW YEAR
COME EARLY AND LEAVE EARLY (at dawn)
"FRONT PAGE" CABARET
HARRY'S NEW YORK BAR
SAY TO DRIVER: SANK ROO DOE NOO.

ANNOUNCEMENTS
Hello Everybody! Merry Xmas!
Miss Repeal and Mister. Volstead have arrived at HARRY'S NEW YORK BAR and will be raffled off tonight.
CABARET — FIREWORKS AND CRACKERS
Say to Driver: Sank Roo Doe Noo.

I AM SAILING TOMORROW
AND I HAVE JUST DROPPED IN
TO SAY GOOD BYE TO ALL THE FRIENDS
I MET THERE, SO BE ON TIME.
HARRY'S NEW YORK BAR
5 RUE DAUNOU (Opera District).
Bar Open All Day and Night. Cabaret 10 P.M.

WASN'T THE DEPRESSION AWFUL!
CELEBRATE "THANKSGIVING"
TURKEY AND HOT TOM AND JERRY
FREE!
WHERE?
Why at "HARRY'S" of course
say to driver sank Roo Doe Noo.

CELEBRATE THE "REPEAL"
AS MUCH CHAMPAGNE AS YOU CAN
DRINK BETWEEN 10 P.M. AND 2 A.M.
50 FRANCS
Book your table now. — Tel.: Opera 73-00.
HARRY'S NEW YORK BAR
("FRONT PAGE" CABARET)
SAY TO DRIVER SANK ROO DOE NOO.

HARRY'S
"FRONT PAGE" CABARET
5, RUE DAUNOU, PARIS
ROY BARTON and BILL HENLY entertain
HARRY'S, 45, Rue St.-Jean, LE TOUQUET
Mlle. Marie JANYL and Glover COMPTON
entertain every evening.

STOP PRESS NEWS
HARRY OF 5 RUE DAUNOU
Presents His New Cabaret Downstairs
The 'FRONT PAGE'
TONIGHT !! TONIGHT !!

ONLY AMERICAN CABARET IN TOWN
ROY BARTON (New York)
GLOVER (Chicago)
entertain every evening, 10 o'clock.
HARRY'S NEW YORK BAR
say to driver sank roo doe noo.
BAR OPEN ALL DAY AND NIGHT.

"SCHNITZELBANK"
SUNG NIGHTLY AT 5 RUE DAUNOU
HARRY'S NEW YORK BAR
"FRONT PAGE" CABARET
BARTON & HENLY ENTERTAIN
HARRY'S AT LE TOUQUET
CABARET EVERY NIGHT
GLOVER AND MLLE. JANYL ENTERTAIN

BOOK YOUR TABLE NOW
INAUGURATION BROADCAST
HARRY'S NEW YORK BAR, PARIS.
NOTE: TABLES NOT OCCUPIED
BEFORE 4 P.M. NOT GUARANTEED.
HARRY.

HARRY'S BAR
5, RUE DAUNOU (OPERA), PARIS.
Mlle. JANYL and ROY BARTON
sing every evening 10 p.m.

TONIGHT! TONIGHT!
CELEBRATE THE "REPEAL"
AS MUCH CHAMPAGNE YOU CAN DRINK
between 10 p.m. to 2 a.m.
50 FRANCS
HARRY'S NEW YORK BAR
("FRONT PAGE" CABARET)
SAY TO DRIVER: SANK ROO DOE NOO.

HARRY'S. Bass on tap. Snacks. Say to driver, "Sank Roo Doenoo," and expect the worst.

1. Das Café de Paris, London / *The Café de Paris, London.*
2. Die Rivoli Bar, London / *The Rivoli Bar, London.*
3. Henry (Mac), Harrys ältester Sohn, trifft nach seiner Flucht in London ein / *Henry (Mac), Harry's eldest son, arrives in London after his escape*

RUN AWAY!

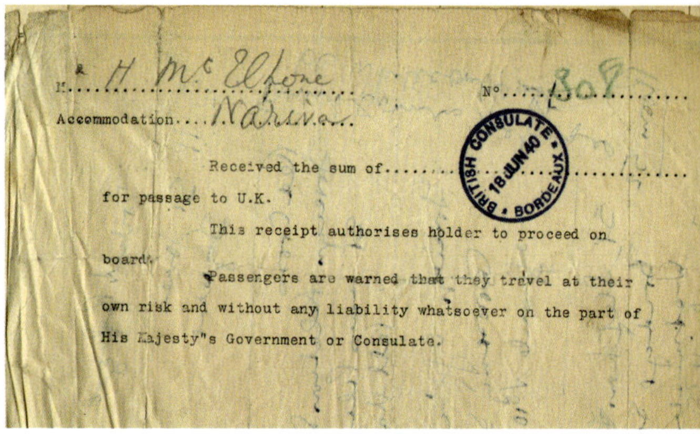
M. H Mc Elhone No. 808
Accommodation....Nariva....
Received the sum of.......................................
for passage to U.K.
This receipt authorises holder to proceed on board.
Passengers are warned that they travel at their own risk and without any liability whatsoever on the part of His Majesty's Government or Consulate.

RETTE SICH, WER KANN!

Als der Zweite Weltkrieg ausbrach, war Harry schon zu alt und sein Sohn Andrew noch zu jung, um zum Militärdienst eingezogen zu werden. Harrys ältester Sohn Henry, Mac genannt, wurde zur französischen Armee einberufen.

Die Bar blieb zwar geöffnet, doch die Geschäfte gingen schlecht. Die Amerikaner, die 1929 noch nicht gegangen waren, bekamen es nun mit der Angst zu tun und verließen 1938 und 1939 in Scharen die Stadt. Eines Tages im Juni 1940 erfuhr Harry, dass die Deutschen Belgien überrannt und Dünkirchen eingenommen hatten. Er sah, wie Andrew überlieferte, »eine Horde Touristen auf Motorrädern, die alle gleich angezogen waren«, und erkannte, dass es Zeit war, die Stadt zu verlassen. Er mauerte schnell den hochprozentigen Alkohol im Keller ein und verstaute seine Maskottchen und Erinnerungsstücke in seinem Haus in Garches, außerhalb von Paris. Dann packte er seinen Sohn Andrew und einige Flaschen Champagner in seinen Topolino, den er noch hatte auftanken können, und machte sich auf den Weg nach Bordeaux. Doch kaum hatte er die Loire überquert, gab der Motor den Geist auf. Harry überließ das restliche Benzin einem Lastwagenfahrer, der keinen Sprit mehr hatte und Harry dafür nach Bordeaux schleppte. Da auch die Bremsen des Topolino kaputt waren, fuhr Harry bei jedem Bremsmanöver auf den Lastwagen auf. Erschöpft erreichten Vater und Sohn Bordeaux und schafften es gerade noch auf ein Schiff, das nach London auslief. Die Überfahrt dauerte zwölf Stunden. Am 18. Juni 1940 kam Harry in Falmouth in Cornwall, Südwestengland, an.

Hallo **London**

Harry und Andrew kamen nach London, wo sie Arbeit im Café de Paris fanden, einem sehr eleganten Nachtklub. Dass Krieg war, hieß nicht, dass man in London nicht feiern konnte. Harry reagierte auf die Situation, indem er zwei neue Cocktails kreierte: den *Hurricane* und den *Spitfire*, eine Hommage an die Jagdflugzeuge der Royal Air Force. Eines Abends wurde das Viertel von der Luftwaffe bombardiert. Wie durch ein Wunder blieben Harry und Andrew fast unversehrt, doch der Club wurde vollständig zerstört. Im November 1940 wurde Harry Manager einer neuen amerikanischen Bar im nahe gelegenen Hotel Ritz. Weil die Straße, an der die Bar lag, der Rue de Rivoli in Paris ähnelte, nannte Harry sie kurzerhand Rivoli Bar. Harrys Ruf und der seiner Pariser Bar war ihm längst über den Kanal vorausgeeilt, sodass etliche Diplomaten aus von deutschen Truppen besetzten Ländern im Ritz verkehrten, wo Harry drei neue Cocktails erfand: den *Mustang*, den *Ranger* und den *Commando*. Die Rivoli Bar gehört noch heute zu den beliebtesten Bars in London.

Während eines Luftangriffs ging auch ein Manuskript verloren, das Harry in Paris verfasst hatte. Nach seiner Ankunft in London hatte er es an den Verlag Hutchinson's geschickt, der bereits sein Büchlein *ABC of Mixing Cocktails* veröffentlicht hatte. Doch das Gebäude wurde getroffen, und alles darin, einschließlich der Manuskripte, ging in Flammen auf. Harry hatte nicht die Kraft, mit dem Schreiben noch einmal von vorn anzufangen.

1.

2.

3.

When WWII broke out, Harry was too old to be mobilized, and his son Andrew too young to fight. Harry's eldest son, Henry, nicknamed Mac, was called up by the French army and was posted to the Maginot Line.

The bar stayed open, but business was, obviously, not flourishing. Those members of the American community who had not left in 1929 took fright and fled in 1938-1939. One day in June 1940, Harry learned that the Germans had crossed Belgium and taken Dunkirk. And when he saw, in his own words as reported by his son Andrew, "a pack of tourists on motor bikes all dressed the same," he realized that it was high time he left the capital. He quickly took his strong liquor down to the cellar, bricked it up and stowed his mascots and memorabilia in a safe place in his home in Garches, just outside Paris. Then he drove off with Andrew and a few bottles of champagne in his Topolino (the original of the Fiat 500), which he had been able to fill up with gasoline, and headed towards Bordeaux. But just after they crossed the Loire, the car's engine gave up. Harry bartered the remainder of his gasoline with a truck-driver who had run out of gas for a tow to Bordeaux. The Topolino's brakes had also failed, so each time the truck braked, the Topolino crashed into its rear. Exhausted, father and son arrived in Bordeaux just as a ship destined for London was about to leave. The crossing lasted twelve hours, and on 18 June 1940, Harry landed at Falmouth, in Cornwall, South West England.

Hello **London**

When they arrived in London, Harry and Andrew found work at the Café de Paris, an extremely elegant night spot with cabaret acts and a band – the war was no reason not to have fun in London. Harry responded to the situation by creating two new cocktails, the Hurricane and Spitfire, as a tribute to the pilots of the Royal Air Force and their fighter aircraft. One evening, the neighborhood came under aerial bombardment. By a miracle neither father nor son was seriously injured, but the club was completely destroyed. In November 1940, Harry was appointed manager of a new American bar in the nearby Ritz Hotel. Because the street the bar gave on to resembled Rue de Rivoli in Paris, he called it the Rivoli Bar. Harry's reputation, and that of Harry's Bar, had already crossed the Channel, and crowds of diplomats from countries occupied by Nazi Germany came to find Harry in his bar at the Ritz, where he invented three new cocktails: the Mustang, the Ranger and the Commando. The Rivoli Bar is still a favorite meeting place in London.

It was during an air raid that the manuscript of Harry's memoirs, which he had written in Paris, disappeared. When Harry had arrived in London, he had sent the manuscript to Hutchinson's, which had already published his *ABC of Mixing Cocktails*. But following the air raid, the building caught fire, and everything in it went up in flames, including his manuscript. Harry didn't have the strength to begin writing all over again.

THE "**LIBERATION**" OF **HARRY'S** BAR

DIE **»BEFREIUNG«** VON HARRY'S BAR

Doch was geschah in der Zwischenzeit mit Harry's Bar? Sie wurde als »feindliches Eigentum« requiriert. Den Informationen nach hatte die Pariser Handelskammer ihr einen Manager zugeteilt, und mit Ausnahme von Charlie Soumille waren die Barkeeper aus der Stadt geflohen.

Im Dezember 1941 trat Amerika offiziell in den Krieg gegen Deutschland ein. Bis dahin verkehrten einige Amerikaner in der Bar auch mit jungen deutschen Offizieren, die zum Teil Universitäten in den USA oder Großbritannien besucht hatten und gern Englisch sprachen.

Der Humorist Yvan Audouard berichtete in einem Artikel, der 1958 in der *Paris-Presse* veröffentlicht wurde: *Während der Besatzung sind amerikanische Piloten, die über unserem Gebiet abgeschossen worden waren, in Harry's Bar gekommen, um den Duft von Whiskey und Freiheit zu schnuppern.*

Nach seiner Flucht aus dem Kriegsgefangenenlager kam Harrys ältester Sohn Henry, der sich nun den Kämpfern der Résistance anschließen wollte, nach Paris. Er rief in der Bar an, um zu fragen, was mit den Alkoholvorräten geschehen war, die sein Vater versteckt hatte, und erfuhr, dass alles noch an Ort und Stelle war. Auch Andrew konnte mit guten Neuigkeiten aufwarten. Einem seiner Freunde, der wie er für den britischen Geheimdienst arbeitete und gerade einen Spionageauftrag im besetzten Frankreich erledigte, war es gelungen, die Bar zu fotografieren. Alles war noch intakt bis auf das Namensschild, das jemand glücklicherweise entfernt hatte. Sonst hätten womöglich die Deutschen wegen des Schriftzugs »Harry's New York Bar« deren Zerstörung angeordnet.

1944 wurde Harry's Bar von seiner Tochter Patricia »befreit«. Sie arbeitete für das amerikanische Rote Kreuz und kam kurz nach der Befreiung von Paris in die französische Hauptstadt. Dort wurde sie dem Management des Grand Hôtel in der Rue Scribe zugeteilt, die nicht weit von der Bar entfernt ist. Das Hotel diente der US-Armee als Unterkunft für Soldaten auf Fronturlaub, genau wie es vorher zur Unterbringung deutscher Soldaten benutzt worden war. Patricia ging in die »Sank Roo Doe Noo« und fand die Türen verschlossen vor. Der Manager hatte die Bar nach der Befreiung von Paris geschlossen. Patricia kontaktierte die früheren Barkeeper Henri Kepe, Robert, Émile Dumont, Charlie Soumille und Edouard, und Ende 1944 machten sie gemeinsam die Bar wieder auf.

Die Wiedereröffnung war vor allem eine symbolische Geste, da es kaum mehr Vorräte gab. Denn die Deutschen hatten vor ihrem Abzug die Backsteinmauer im Keller eingerissen und alles mitgenommen, was Harry dort versteckt hatte. Wundersamerweise jedoch hatten sie die teuren Whiskys, die Harry in einer Glasvitrine gegenüber der Bar aufbewahrte, nicht angerührt. Wahrscheinlich hatten sie gedacht, die Flaschen seien nur Attrappen. Doch das Klavier im Keller war auch verschwunden.

Die Bar, die einstweilen nur mit Kerzen und Öllampen beleuchtet wurde, konnte nicht länger als ein paar Stunden am Tag – von 17.00 bis 19.00 Uhr – öffnen. Doch die Gäste kamen gern zurück und waren froh, dass sie durch den Krieg nicht zu arg gelitten hatte. Trotz des Mangels an Alkohol gelang es den früheren Lieferanten, die Bar mit einigen Flaschen Cognac und Wermut zu bestücken.

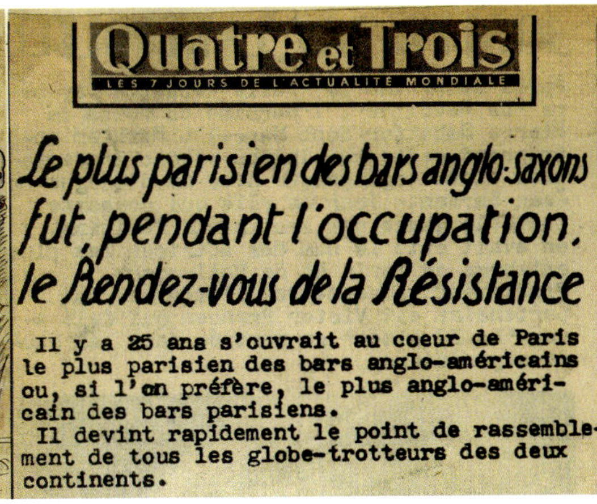

Quatre et Trois

LES 7 JOURS DE L'ACTUALITE MONDIALE

Le plus parisien des bars anglo-saxons fut, pendant l'occupation, le Rendez-vous de la Résistance

Il y a 25 ans s'ouvrait au coeur de Paris le plus parisien des bars anglo-américains ou, si l'on préfère, le plus anglo-américain des bars parisiens.
Il devint rapidement le point de rassemblement de tous les globe-trotteurs des deux continents.

72

NEW YORK HERALD TRIBUNE, PARIS,
WEDNESDAY, APRIL 18, 1945

Harry's Back
AT
Harry's New York Bar
5 RUE DAUNOU
(Closed Saturday and Sunday)
(Just ask for: SANK ROO DOE NOO)

But what was happening to Harry's Bar, meantime? It was requisitioned as an "Enemy Asset". The Paris Chamber of Commerce is said to have appointed a manager and the barmen are thought to have taken refuge outside the capital, except for just one of them, Charlie Soumille.

In December 1941, the United States officially entered the war against Germany. Until then, the Bar had been frequented by a few Americans who rubbed shoulders with young German officers, some of whom had attended leading US or British universities and who liked to speak English.

The humorist Yvan Audouard, in an article published in *Paris-Presse* in 1958, reported that, "During the Occupation, American airmen who had been shot down over our territory used to come to Harry's to smell the perfume of whisky and the aroma of freedom."

After escaping from a prisoner of war camp, Harry's elder son Henry passed through Paris on his way to join the Free French forces. He telephoned the Bar to find out what had happened to the stash of spirits his father had hidden, and learned that it was still intact. Next it was Andrew's turn to provide good news. One of his friends (like him, a member of the British secret service) on a spying assignment in occupied France managed to take a photo of the Bar. Everything was still in place, except the street sign, which someone had fortunately removed, thereby avoiding the risk that a German officer, seeing "Harry's New York Bar" painted in the entrance, might assume it was an American establishment and order its destruction.

In 1944, Harry's Bar was "liberated" by Harry's daughter, Patricia. A member of the American Red Cross, she arrived in the French capital shortly after the Liberation of Paris. She was posted to the management of the Grand Hôtel, in nearby Rue Scribe, which had been requisitioned for American soldiers on furlough, just as it had previously been used to accommodate German soldiers. Patricia went to *Sank Roo Doe Noo* but found the doors closed. The manager had shut the Bar when Paris was liberated. She managed to contact the former barmen, Henri Kepe, Robert, Émile Dumont, Charlie Soumille and Edouard. All answered the call, and together, at the end of 1944, they reopened the Bar.

But the reopening was a largely symbolic gesture as there was no stock. Before they retreated from Paris, the Germans had demolished the brick wall in the cellar and taken everything that Harry had hidden there. On the other hand, by some unexplained miracle, they had not touched the precious whiskies Harry kept in a glass case facing the bar, such as the pure malt Glenlivet, the John Haig Gold Label and the Lem Motlow's Tennessee Sour Mash Whiskey. They probably thought the bottles were fakes. The piano in the downstairs bar had disappeared, too.

The Bar, lit by a few candles and oil lamps, could only open a couple of hours a day, from 5 to 7 p.m., but the customers came, happy to return to a favorite watering hole and to see that it had not suffered too much from the war. Despite the shortage of spirits, the Bar's former suppliers managed to deliver a few bottles of cognac and vermouth.

1. Jack »Bumby« Hemingway signierte dieses Foto für Andrew / *Jack "Bumby" Hemingway autographed this photo for Andrew.*
2. Max Douy rekonstruierte Harry's Bar in den Saint-Maurice-Filmstudios für den Film *Der Teufel im Leib* von Claude Autant-Lara / *Max Douy recreated Harry's Bar at the Saint-Maurice film studios for the set of* Devil in the Flesh, *by Claude Autant-Lara*
3. Seite 58 »Avec le Sourire«, eine Unterhaltungsshow, moderiert von Catherine Joubert, wurde ab und zu aus Harry's Bar gesendet / "Avec le sourire", a variety show compered by Catherine Joubert, was occasionally set in Harry's Bar.
4. Seite 61 Der französische Schauspieler Edouard Baer in Harry's Bar in Paris am Tag der amerikanischen Präsidentschaftswahl 2008 / *French actor Edouard Baer at Harry's Bar in Paris, Election Day, 2008*
5. Seite 61 Juliette Greco in Harry's Bar in Paris / *Juliette Greco at Harry's Bar in Paris.*

1.

NEW GENERATIONS

NEUE GENERATIONEN

Die ersten Amerikaner, die nach dem Krieg in Harry's Bar strömten, um die Befreiung von Paris mit Stil zu feiern, waren GIs. Die Stammgäste aus der Zeit vor dem Krieg schauten ab und an vorbei, wenn sie zu Besuch in Paris waren.

Auch Ernest Hemingway, der ein loyaler Freund war, vergewisserte sich persönlich, dass es Harry's Bar noch gab. Er hatte zuletzt in den Dreißigerjahren in Paris gelebt, kam aber in regelmäßigen Abständen zurück. Seine Freundschaft mit Harry und die glücklichen Zeiten in der Bar waren ihm in herzlicher Erinnerung geblieben. 1948 tauchte Hemingways Sohn Jack (Bumby), mit dem Andrew einen Teil seiner Kindheit verbracht hatte, gemeinsam mit seinen Töchtern in der Bar auf. Und die Besuche gingen weiter. Jeder, der Harry's Bar kannte, kam irgendwann wieder. *Sank Roo Doe Noo* blieb eine Anlaufstelle.

Das Jahr 1955 brachte eine historische Wende im Transatlantikverkehr: Erstmals reisten mehr Leute auf dem Luft- als auf dem Wasserweg. Dessen ungeachtet kamen weniger Amerikaner nach Frankreich als in der Zwischenkriegszeit. In der Folge mussten die amerikanischen Bars im Opéra-Viertel eine nach der anderen schließen. Auch Harry's Bar war gezwungen, sich anzupassen. Obwohl Andrew MacElhone weder das Dekor der Bar noch den Modus Operandi änderte, suchte er doch nach einer breiteren Stammkundschaft.

Literatur und Seventh Art in Harry's Bar

1947 wurde Harry's Bar zum Schauplatz eines Films. Der Raum wurde in den Saint-Maurice-Studios im Osten von Paris nachgebaut, wo Claude Autant-Lara seinen Film *Der Teufel im Leib* mit Micheline Presle and Gérard Philipe drehte. Im folgenden Jahrzehnt wurde die Bar Teil einer Radiosendung. Wally Phillips, Moderator des Chicagoer Senders *WGN*, machte dort ein- oder zweimal im Monat eine Liveshow mit Andrew, bei der über die neuesten Nachrichten und Klatschgeschichten aus Paris geplauscht wurde. In den Sechzigerjahren diente Harry's Bar oft als Set für Werbeaufnahmen, in erster Linie für Laboratoires Garnier, und für Modeaufnahmen für das Magazin *Elle*, und auch heute finden dort noch zahlreiche Fotoshoots statt.

2.

After the war, GIs were the first Americans to flock to Harry's Bar to celebrate the Liberation of Paris in style. The regulars from before the war went back from time to time when they visited France. Ernest Hemingway, a loyal friend, made sure that Harry's Bar was still there. He had not lived in France since the thirties but came back at frequent intervals. He had very warm memories of his friendship with Harry and the truly happy times he had spent in the Bar. In 1948, Hemingway's son, Jack ("Bumby") Hemingway, with whom Andrew had spent part of his childhood, turned up at the Bar with his daughters. The visits never stopped. Anyone who had once known Harry's Bar goes back whenever the opportunity arises. *Sank Roo Doe Noo* had become an essential port of call for anyone who had ever frequented the Bar.

In 1955 came a historic change for the Americans who crossed the Atlantic: for the first time that year, more people made the journey by air than by sea. Despite this, they travelled less frequently to France than they did between the wars. The American bars in the Opéra neighborhood shut down one after the other. Harry's Bar had to adapt, and Andrew MacElhone, without changing the décor, nor its modus operandi, sought a more diversified customer base.

Literature and the Seventh Art at Harry's Bar

In 1947, Harry's Bar starred in a film. Its décor was recreated on a set at the Saint-Maurice studios in Eastern Paris for the filming of Claude Autant-Lara's *Le Diable au corps* (*The Devil in the Flesh*), starring Micheline Presle and Gérard Philipe. During the next decade, Harry's Bar was featured on the radio. Wally Phillips, a famous announcer for WGN, a Chicago radio station, broadcast a live program there once or twice a month with Andrew, where they talked about the latest news and gossip from Paris.

In the 1960s, Harry's Bar was often used as a setting for advertising photo shoots (notably for the Laboratoires Garnier) and fashion shoots for *Elle* magazine. Even today, Harry's Bar is still a popular shooting venue.

TELE-CINE REVELATI

TV ciné actualité

TV

LUNDI 8 JUIN. 20 H. 35

la télévision entre au Harry's

Le Harry's Bar qui servira cette semaine de cadre à l'émission de Jacqueline Joubert « Avec le sourire », fut le Café de Flore de l'époque 1920-1929. On était sûr d'y rencontrer alors tous les soirs Hemingway, Scott Fitzgerald le désenchanté, la championne de tennis Suzanne Lenglen entourée des Dolly Sisters, de Gershwin ou d'Henry Miller, sans compter William Faulkner, Cole Porter et Gertrude Stein.

Aujourd'hui, beaucoup de ces noms célèbres ont disparu. On peut surtout y voir Hemingway (encore lui), à chacun de ses passages à Paris, le metteur en scène Preston Sturges, les écrivains Thornton Wilder et John Steinbeck et aussi une certaine catégorie de buveurs plus connus sous le nom d'I.B.F. (les International Bar Flies, en français : l'Association des Piliers de Bar).

3.

Darüber hinaus wurde die Bar erneut zum Hauptquartier der Presse. In den Nachkriegsjahren war Paris für amerikanische Journalisten das Medienzentrum Europas. Während in den USA McCarthys Hexenjagd in vollem Gange war, konnten sie in Frankreich ihre Meinung frei äußern. Häufige Gäste waren Larry Collins, Korrespondent der *United Press* und Autor des Buches *Is Paris Burning?*, sowie später Bill Granger von der *Chicago Tribune*. Journalisten trafen sich dort auch oft mit Prominenten, über die sie berichteten.

Der zunehmende Einfluss des Fernsehens wirkte sich nachteilig auf einige amerikanische Zeitungen aus, die in der Folge ihre Büros in Paris schließen mussten. Die Fernsehsender, die stattdessen kamen, brauchten weniger Personal, sodass die Zahl der amerikanischen Gäste in Harry's Bar weiter sank. 1953 bestückte Harry die Bar mit einem Fernsehapparat, damit alle die Krönung Königin Elisabeths II. verfolgen konnten. Doch da in den ersten zehn Minuten der Übertragung weder jemand sprach noch ein Glas leerte, schaltete Harry den Fernseher als geschäftsschädigend wieder ab. Danach wurde er nur noch eingeschaltet, um die Ergebnisse amerikanischer Präsidentschaftswahlen zu erfahren.

Wenngleich Harry's Bar auch im Fernsehen vorkam, vor allem als Kulisse einer Show namens *Avec le sourire* (Mit einem Lächeln) mit Jacqueline Joubert, taucht sie doch eher in der Literatur auf. Viele amerikanische Schriftsteller haben sie entweder als Schauplatz der Handlung oder als Bezugspunkt für ein bestimmtes Ereignis benutzt. In den Zwischenkriegsjahren wurde sie in Ernest Hemingways Roman *Fiesta* (1926) erwähnt: *Vor drei Tagen hatte Harvey mir beim Würfelpoker in der New York Bar zweihundert Franc abgenommen.* Desgleichen auch in Sinclair Lewis' Roman *Sam Dodsworth* (1929) und in Wythe Williams' Buch *Dusk of Empire* (1937). Nach dem Zweiten Weltkrieg kam sie in *Tell Sparta* von A. C. Sedgwick (1945) vor, in *Paris Was Our Mistress* von Samuel Putman (1945), *We Were Interrupted* von Burton Rascoe (1947), *An Affair of State* von Pat Frank (1948), *Suitable for Framing* von James Atlee Phillips (1949), *Der Entzauberte* von Budd Schulberg (1950) und in vielen weiteren Geschichten, darunter Ian Flemings *For Your Eyes Only* (1960), in der James Bond der Bar einen Besuch abstattet. Harry's Bar findet außerdem Erwähnung in einigen Reiseführern. Einer der ersten war *The Paris That's Not In The Guide Books* von Basil Woon (1926), und Bruce Reynolds' *Paris with the Lid Lifted* (1927).

Harry's Bar ist ebenso legendär wie ihre Gäste. Amerikanische Künstler haben sich dort immer zu Hause gefühlt und durch ihre Anwesenheit der Bar zu Prominenz und einem breiteren Publikum verholfen. Leinwandstars verkehren dort bis zum heutigen Tag. Manche waren Stammgäste, ohne in Paris zu leben, so Gene Kelly, Noel Coward, Rex Harrison und Marlene Dietrich. Andere kamen seltener, wie Gregory Peck, Gloria Swanson und Charlie Chaplin. Schriftsteller

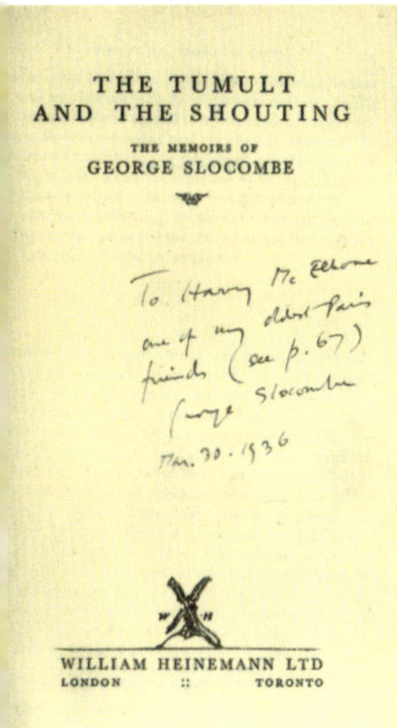

THE TUMULT AND THE SHOUTING

THE MEMOIRS OF GEORGE SLOCOMBE

To Harry McElhone
one of my oldest Paris
friends (see p. 67)
George Slocombe
Mar. 30. 1936

WILLIAM HEINEMANN LTD
LONDON :: TORONTO

THE SUN ALSO RISES

By

Ernest Hemingway

ZEPHYR BOOKS

The Continental Book Company AB
STOCKHOLM/LONDON

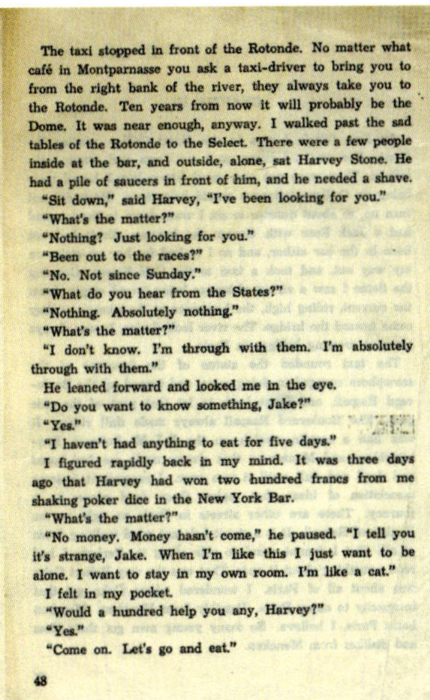

The taxi stopped in front of the Rotonde. No matter what café in Montparnasse you ask a taxi-driver to bring you to from the right bank of the river, they always take you to the Rotonde. Ten years from now it will probably be the Dome. It was near enough, anyway. I walked past the sad tables of the Rotonde to the Select. There were a few people inside at the bar, and outside, alone, sat Harvey Stone. He had a pile of saucers in front of him, and he needed a shave.

"Sit down," said Harvey, "I've been looking for you."

"What's the matter?"

"Nothing? Just looking for you."

"Been out to the races?"

"No. Not since Sunday."

"What do you hear from the States?"

"Nothing. Absolutely nothing."

"What's the matter?"

"I don't know. I'm through with them. I'm absolutely through with them."

He leaned forward and looked me in the eye.

"Do you want to know something, Jake?"

"Yes."

"I haven't had anything to eat for five days."

I figured rapidly back in my mind. It was three days ago that Harvey had won two hundred francs from me shaking poker dice in the New York Bar.

"What's the matter?"

"No money. Money hasn't come," he paused. "I tell you it's strange, Jake. When I'm like this I just want to be alone. I want to stay in my own room. I'm like a cat."

I felt in my pocket.

"Would a hundred help you any, Harvey?"

"Yes."

"Come on. Let's go and eat."

48

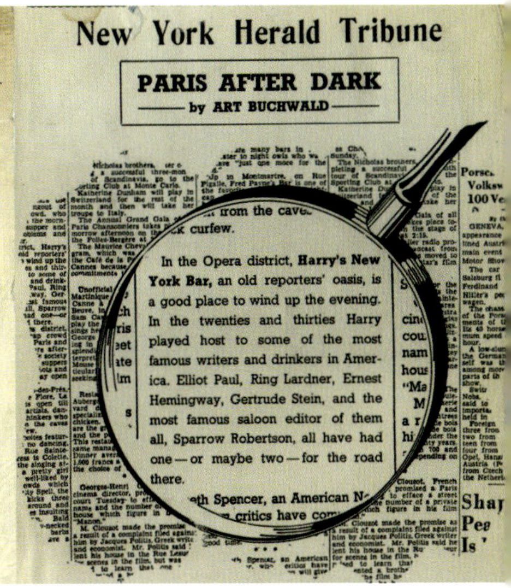

New York Herald Tribune

PARIS AFTER DARK

by ART BUCHWALD

In the Opera district, **Harry's New York Bar,** an old reporters' oasis, is a good place to wind up the evening. In the twenties and thirties Harry played host to some of the most famous writers and drinkers in America. Elliot Paul, Ring Lardner, Ernest Hemingway, Gertrude Stein, and the most famous saloon editor of them all, Sparrow Robertson, all have had one—or maybe two—for the road there.

The press turned it into their HQ. In the post-war years, Paris was seen by American journalists as the hub for European news, and with the McCarthy witch-hunt in full force in the United States, many came to France to find the freedom of expression missing back home. Harry's Bar thus became, once more, the center of intensive journalistic activity. Larry Collins, a correspondent for *United Press* and author of *Is Paris Burning?*, and later Bill Granger of the *Chicago Tribune* often came by, and the journalists frequently met the celebrities they would write about at the Bar.

But television was fast becoming a major influence, to the detriment of some American newspapers which closed their French offices. The TV stations that replaced them required fewer staff, leading to a fall-off in American patrons at Harry's. A TV set was installed in 1953 to broadcast the coronation of Queen Elizabeth II of England. But because, ten minutes into the broadcast, no-one had said a word or drunk a single glass, Harry decided to turn off the set, saying it was anti-commercial and anti-social! Thereafter, it was only turned on to broadcast the results of American presidential elections.

Although Harry's Bar was also seen on TV, most notably as the setting for a show by Jacqueline Joubert called *Avec le sourire* ("With a smile"), the Bar features most prominently in literature. It is mentioned in the works of numerous American novelists, either as a setting for the action, or as an essential reference to situate an event. At the end of the 1920s, it rated a mention in Ernest Hemingway's 1926 *The Sun Also Rises* ("It was three days ago that Harvey won two hundred francs from me shaking poker dice in the New York Bar"), in *Dodsworth* by Sinclair Lewis (1929) and in *Dusk of Empire* by Wythe Williams (1937). After WWII it was mentioned in *Tell Sparta* by A.C. Sedgwick (1945), *Paris Was Our Mistress* by Samuel Putnam (1945), *We Were Interrupted* by Burton Rascoe (1947), *An Affair of State* by Pat Frank (1948), *Suitable for Framing* by James Atlee Phillips (1949), *The Disenchanted* by Budd Schulberg (1950) and by many others, including Ian Fleming, who has James Bond stop by Harry's Bar in *For Your Eyes Only* (1960). It is also mentioned in tourist guides, one of the first by Basil Woon, *The Paris That's Not in the Guide Books* (1926), and then *Paris with the Lid Lifted* by Bruce Reynolds (1927).

Harry's Bar is the stuff of legend and is frequented by legendary beings. American artists have always felt at home there, and their presence has contributed to boosting the Bar's fame and expanding its audience. Stars of the silver screen could and still can be seen there, some of whom were regular fixtures, even if they did not live in Paris, such as Gene Kelly, Noël Coward, Rex Harrison and

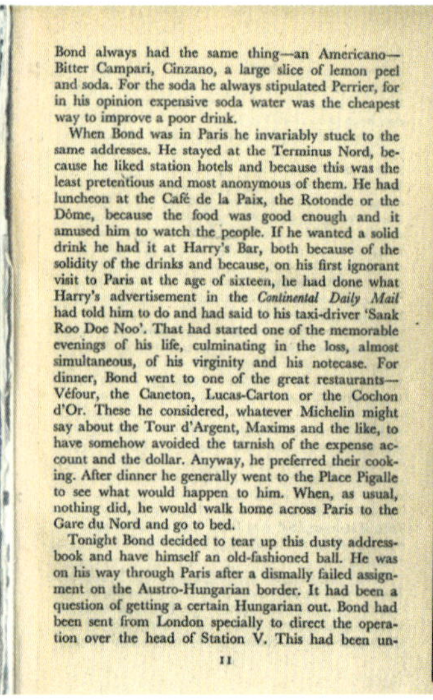

Bond always had the same thing—an Americano—Bitter Campari, Cinzano, a large slice of lemon peel and soda. For the soda he always stipulated Perrier, for in his opinion expensive soda water was the cheapest way to improve a poor drink.

When Bond was in Paris he invariably stuck to the same addresses. He stayed at the Terminus Nord, because he liked station hotels and because this was the least pretentious and most anonymous of them. He had luncheon at the Café de la Paix, the Rotonde or the Dôme, because the food was good enough and it amused him to watch the people. If he wanted a solid drink he had it at Harry's Bar, both because of the solidity of the drinks and because, on his first ignorant visit to Paris at the age of sixteen, he had done what Harry's advertisement in the *Continental Daily Mail* had told him to do and had said to his taxi-driver 'Sank Roo Doe Noo'. That had started one of the memorable evenings of his life, culminating in the loss, almost simultaneous, of his virginity and his notecase. For dinner, Bond went to one of the great restaurants—Véfour, the Caneton, Lucas-Carton or the Cochon d'Or. These he considered, whatever Michelin might say about the Tour d'Argent, Maxims and the like, to have somehow avoided the tarnish of the expense account and the dollar. Anyway, he preferred their cooking. After dinner he generally went to the Place Pigalle to see what would happen to him. When, as usual, nothing did, he would walk home across Paris to the Gare du Nord and go to bed.

Tonight Bond decided to tear up this dusty address-book and have himself an old-fashioned ball. He was on his way through Paris after a dismally failed assignment on the Austro-Hungarian border. It had been a question of getting a certain Hungarian out. Bond had been sent from London specially to direct the operation over the head of Station V. This had been un-

11

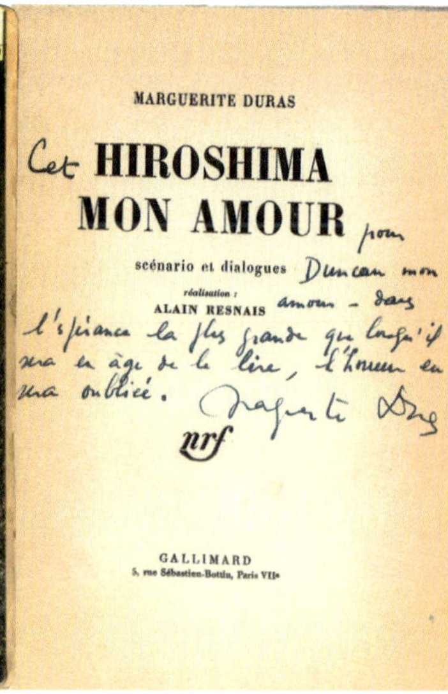

MARGUERITE DURAS

HIROSHIMA MON AMOUR

scénario et dialogues

réalisation : ALAIN RESNAIS

nrf

GALLIMARD
5, rue Sébastien-Bottin, Paris VIIe

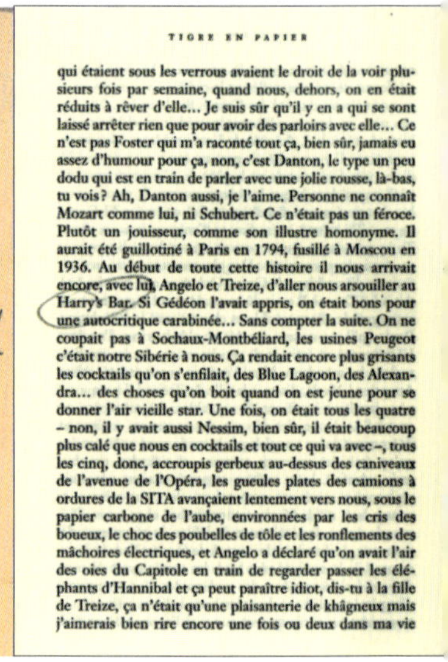

TIGRE EN PAPIER

qui étaient sous les verrous avaient le droit de la voir plusieurs fois par semaine, quand nous, dehors, on en était réduits à rêver d'elle… Je suis sûr qu'il y en a qui se sont laissé arrêter rien que pour avoir des parloirs avec elle… Ce n'est pas Foster qui m'a raconté tout ça, bien sûr, jamais eu assez d'humour pour ça, non, c'est Danton, le type un peu dodu qui est en train de parler avec une jolie rousse, là-bas, tu vois ? Ah, Danton aussi, je l'aime. Personne ne connaît Mozart comme lui, ni Schubert. Ce n'était pas un féroce. Plutôt un jouisseur, comme son illustre homonyme. Il aurait été guillotiné à Paris en 1794, fusillé à Moscou en 1936. Au début de toute cette histoire il nous arrivait encore, avec lui, Angelo et Treize, d'aller nous arsouiller au Harry's Bar. Si Gédéon l'avait appris, on était bons pour une autocritique carabinée… Sans compter la suite. On ne coupait pas à Sochaux-Montbéliard, les usines Peugeot c'était notre Sibérie à nous. Ça rendait encore plus grisants les cocktails qu'on s'enfilait, des Blue Lagoon, des Alexandra… des choses qu'on boit quand on est jeune pour se donner l'air vieille star. Une fois, on était tous les quatre – non, il y avait aussi Nessim, bien sûr, il était beaucoup plus calé que nous en cocktails et tout ce qui va avec –, tous les cinq, donc, accroupis gerbeux au-dessus des caniveaux de l'avenue de l'Opéra, les gueules plates des camions à ordures de la SITA avançaient lentement vers nous, sous le papier carbone de l'aube, environnées par les cris des boueux, le choc des poubelles de tôle et les ronflements des mâchoires électriques, et Angelo a déclaré qu'on avait l'air des oies du Capitole en train de regarder passer les éléphants d'Hannibal et ça peut paraître idiot, dis-tu à la fille de Treize, ça n'était qu'une plaisanterie de khâgneux mais j'aimerais bien rire encore une fois ou deux dans ma vie

aber waren wohl die treuesten Gäste. Dazu gehörten unter anderem Liam O'Flaherty, Cornelius Ryan (*A Bridge too Far*), Brendan Behan, William Saroyan und William Faulkner. Auch der Weltkriegsheld General Dwight D. Eisenhower, der von der Bar und ihrem Flair fasziniert war, kam in die *Sank Roo Doe Noo*, kurz bevor er zum 34. Präsidenten der Vereinigten Staaten gewählt wurde.

Die französischen Drehbuchautoren Jacques Prévert und Marcel Achard, der Humorist Yvan Audouard (ein angesehenes Mitglied des IBF) und schließlich Henri Jeanson, der Autor des Films *Fanfan, der Husar*, waren schon in den Dreißigerjahren Fans von Harry's Bar. Michèle Morgan und Leslie Caron waren ebenfalls oft gesehene Gäste. Manchmal kamen sie auch in Begleitung des Schauspielers Pierre Brasseur. Ihnen folgten bald Jean-Paul Sartre und Simone de Beauvoir, die ungeachtet ihres zur Schau getragenen Anti-Amerikanismus diese Form amerikanischer Lebensart zu schätzen wussten, aber auch Roger Nimier, Antoine Blondin, Marguerite Duras und Kléber Haedens, der in seinem Roman *Adios*[8] von 1974 Harry's Bar folgendermaßen beschreibt: *Ich wartete immer in Harry's Bar auf Marie-Louise und träumte unter Primo Carneras Boxhandschuhen vor mich hin … An manchen Tagen kam ich rasch in der Bar vorbei, in der Banknoten aus aller Welt hingen und Whiskeys, die vor fünfzig Jahren verschwunden waren, in den Glasvitrinen dösten. Nachmittags war es ruhig bei Harry, und ich konnte ungestört meine Schreibarbeit erledigen.*

Man konnte außerdem Jeanne Moreau, Simone Signoret und Jean Gabin begegnen, wie auch dem Filmkritiker und Regisseur Pierre Kast, und selbst einige treue Anhänger der Existenzialisten von Saint-Germain-des-Prés, wie Boris Vian und Juliette Gréco, zählten zu den Stammgästen. Andere, wie die Schriftsteller Françoise Sagan und Lucien Bodard sowie die Schauspielerlegenden Louis Jouvet und Michel Simon, tauchten etwas unregelmäßiger auf.

Auch Anfang des 21. Jahrhunderts wird Harry's Bar noch von bekannten Autoren erwähnt, etwa von François Weyergans in seinem Roman *Drei Tage bei meiner Mutter* (2006)[9]. Didier Van Cauwelaert[10], Olivier Rolin[11] und Antoine Laurain[12] haben Harry's Bar ebenfalls in ihren Romanen verewigt.

Heute zählen zu den Stammgästen unter anderem Étienne Daho, Julie Depardieu, Quentin Tarantino, Guy Bedos, Morgan Freeman, der unbedingt nach dem Filmfestival in Deauville über Paris fahren wollte, nur um einen Abstecher zu Harry's Bar machen zu können, Jean-Charles de Castelbajac, Agnès B, Zazie, Sofia Coppola, Valérie Lemercier und Zoe Cassavetes.

8. Grasset, 1974, Seite 292.
9. Grasset, 2005, Seite 39–42.
10. *Corps étranger*, 2000, Éditions Albin Michel.
11. *Tigre en papier*, 2002, Le Seuil, Seite 71 und 117.
12. *Fume et tue*, 2008, und *Le Carrefour des nostalgies*, 2009, Éditions du Passage.

4.

5.

Marlene Dietrich. Others visited less often. These included Gregory Peck, Gloria Swanson and Charlie Chaplin. But writers have possibly been the most assiduous patrons. Among their number were Liam O'Flaherty, Cornelius (*A Bridge Too Far*) Ryan, Brendan Behan, William Saroyan, William Faulkner and others. General Dwight D. Eisenhower, intrigued by the place, visited *Sank Roo Doe Noo* shortly before becoming the 34th President of the United States.

French screenwriters Jacques Prévert and Marcel Achard, humorist Yvan Audouard (an eminent member of the I.B.F.) and the scriptwriter of *Fanfan la Tulipe*, Henri Jeanson, were early aficionados of Harry's Bar in the 1930s. Michèle Morgan and Leslie Caron were regulars, too, sometimes accompanied by actor Pierre Brasseur. They were soon joined by Jean-Paul Sartre and Simone de Beauvoir (despite their outward anti-Americanism), Roger Nimier, Antoine Blondin, Marguerite Duras and Kléber Haedens, who, in his 1974 novel *Adios*[8] described Harry's Bar as follows: "I used to wait for Marie-Louise at Harry's Bar, daydreaming under the hanging boxing gloves once worn by Primo Carnera... Some days, I would drop briefly by the bar, papered with banknotes from all over the world, and its display cases filled with slumbering whiskies that had disappeared half a century before. Harry's was quiet in the afternoon, and I could settle there with all my paperwork." You might also see Jeanne Moreau, Simone Signoret and Jean Gabin, along with film critic and director Pierre Kast, and even some of the well-known stalwarts of Saint-Germain-des-Prés, such as Boris Vian and Juliette Gréco, all regulars. Others, such as novelists Françoise Sagan and Lucien Bodard and acting legends Louis Jouvet and Michel Simon, showed up occasionally.

In the early years of the 21st century, well-known authors continue to refer to Harry's Bar. François Weyergans included an amusing paragraph on it in his novel *Trois jours chez ma mère*[9]: "Since mummy still didn't seem ready to go back home, I suggested going for a nightcap at Harry's Bar, which closes late. All the tables were taken, so we stood at the bar, by the door. Delphine had the great idea of ordering hot dogs. I've never been disappointed by the hot dogs at Harry's Bar." Didier Van Cauwelaert[10], Olivier Rolin[11] and Antoine Laurain[12] have also mentioned Harry's Bar in their novels.

8. Grasset, Paris, 1974, p. 292.
9. Grasset, Paris, 2005, pp. 39–42.
10. *Corps étranger*, Albin Michel, Paris, 2000.
11. *Tigre en papier*, Le Seuil, Paris, 2002, pp. 71 and 117.
12. *Fume et tue*, and *Le Carrefour des nostalgies*, Éditions du Passage, Paris, 2008, 2009.

Selbst Adelige kann man in der Bar sehen, beispielsweise Fürst Albert II. von Monaco, der anlässlich der Rugby-Weltmeisterschaft vorbeikam, und ebenso Politiker jeder Couleur. Auch Journalisten pflegen noch ihre traditionelle Vorliebe für die Bar, die sie stets mit offenen Armen willkommen geheißen hat. 2002 hat der Jazzmusiker Gordon Haskell eine wundervolle Hommage an Harry's Bar auf seinem gleichnamigen Album aufgenommen. Claude Berri hat dort eine Szene für seinen Film *Zusammen ist man weniger allein* (2007) nach dem gleichnamigen Roman von Anne Gavalda mit Guillaume Canet und Audrey Tautou in den Hauptrollen gedreht, ebenso wie Laure Charpentier für ihren Film *Gigola* (2011) mit Lou Doillon.

Frenchies

Auch wenn Harry's Bar seit jeher die Anlaufstelle schlechthin für Amerikaner in Paris ist – bis zum heutigen Tag liegen dort jeden Morgen amerikanische Zeitungen aus –, ist die neue Generation weniger trinkfest als die vorhergehenden. Andrew sagte: *Hemingway konnte zwanzig Whiskey Sour hintereinander wegkippen und dann in seinem Hotel wieder an die Arbeit gehen.* Mittlerweile machen die Pariser den Löwenanteil der Gäste aus. Je nach Stimmung und Situation bevorzugen sie entweder die lebhafte Atmosphäre im Erdgeschoss oder die etwas diskretere Pianobar im Souterrain. Ganz besonders schätzen die Besucher an der Bar, dass man sich dort nie allein fühlt. Man kann sich ohne weiteres einem Wildfremden anvertrauen, den man wahrscheinlich nie wiedersehen wird. *Durch die freundliche, offene Atmosphäre ist Harry's Bar perfekt zum Entspannen, sodass man gut reden kann. Es ist fast wie eine Psychotherapie*, schwärmt ein weiblicher Stammgast. Diese Tradition ist sehr alt. Es gibt eine Geschichte, derzufolge eines Abends ein Mann in Harry's Bar kam, *ohne Hose, nur mit Hut und Frack bekleidet. Er zog eine Hundeleine hinter sich her und verlangte einen Hamburger für den kleinen Vierbeiner, den es gar nicht gab. Das Barpersonal tat so, als würde es den Hund füttern, während der Betrunkene immer größere Augen bekam. Am Ende ließ er die Leine fallen und lief hinaus in die Nacht. ›Was macht der Hund?‹, fragte Harry, als der Mann das nächste Mal vorbeikam. ›Ich bin geheilt‹, war die Antwort.*[13]

Frauen in Harry's Bar

Nach dem Zweiten Weltkrieg verteilte Harry ein kleines, nur hundertseitiges Büchlein mit dem Titel *What I Know About Women* (Was ich über Frauen weiß) mit lauter leeren Seiten.

Dabei gab es schon immer viele Frauen unter Harrys Gästen. Und im Gegensatz zu anderen Etablissements, in denen Damen ohne Begleitung freundlich des Hauses verwiesen wurden, hatten sie bei Harry keine Sekunde Grund, sich unwohl zu fühlen, ganz im Gegenteil.

Auch für Frauen war die Bar in der Rue Daunou mit ihrer entspannten Atmosphäre ein »Little America«, wo man sich dank der Mischung aus Jazz, Cocktails und Amerikanern in den wilden Zwanziger auf amerikanische Art amüsieren konnte, ohne die hohen Kosten für die Überfahrt in die Vereinigten Staaten tragen zu müssen.

Heute machen Damen einen guten Teil der Stammgäste aus, wobei es keine Rolle spielt, ob sie mit oder ohne Begleitung erscheinen. Die meisten ziehen jedoch die etwas gemütlichere Pianobar vor. Sie kommen auch gern zum Mittagessen[14] oder am Nachmittag, wenn es ruhiger ist.

Auch eine Reihe von Models sind unter den Gästen. Sie alle haben ihre Lieblings-Barkeeper und sagen während der Modewoche in Paris regelmäßig Hallo. Außerdem wurde die Bar schon wiederholt für Modeaufnahmen benutzt. Auch die Damen, die in Juweliergeschäften, Banken und Anwaltskanzleien rund um den Place Vendôme arbeiten, werden schnell zu Stammgästen. Vielleicht liegt es an der aktuellen »Patronne«, Isabelle MacElhone, dass weiblichen Gästen heute in Harry's Bar besondere Aufmerksamkeit zuteil wird.

13. *The Ocean Press*, 1949
14. Neben den legendären Hot dogs (chiens chauds) gibt es in Harry's Bar jetzt auch leichte Mittagsgerichte. Mittag ist auch die einzige Tageszeit, zu der man Kaffee bestellen kann.

Today, the new regulars include Étienne Daho, Julie Depardieu, Quentin Tarantino, Guy Bedos, Morgan Freeman (who insisted on passing through Paris after the Deauville American Film Festival just so he could stop by Harry's Bar), Jean-Charles de Castelbajac, Agnès B, Zazie, Sofia Coppola, Valérie Lemercier and Zoe Cassavetes. Royalty, too, can be seen there, with Prince Albert II of Monaco dropping in for the Rugby World Cup. Politicians of every persuasion also like to frequent the Bar, and journalists retain their traditional fondness for the place, which has always given them the warmest of welcomes. Jazzman Gordon Haskell recorded a wonderful tribute to Harry's Bar in 2002 with his memorable album of the same name. Claude Berri shot a scene there for his 2007 movie *Ensemble, c'est tout*, adapted from the Anne Gavalda novel, and starring Guillaume Canet and Audrey Tautou. Laure Charpentier filmed a scene from *Gigola* (released in January 2011) there with Lou Doillon.

Frenchies

Although Harry's Bar has always been an essential port of call for Americans in Paris (US newspapers are still delivered there each morning), the new generation is more sober than its predecessors (Andrew said that "Hemingway could down twenty whisky sours in a single visit and then go back to his hotel to work"). Parisians today account for the lion's share of the clientele at Harry's. Depending on their mood and the circumstances, they prefer the lively atmosphere of the ground floor, or the more discreet ambience of the downstairs piano-bar. It's also a place where people like to go because you never feel alone. You can confide in a stranger you will probably never see again. "With its friendly, welcoming character, Harry's Bar is the perfect place to relax, and feel good enough to talk… it's almost psychotherapy," said one female regular. That tradition goes back a long way. There is one story about a man who came to Harry's Bar one night "wearing top hat and tailcoat but no trousers. He was trailing a dog leash and he demanded a hamburger for the little dog who wasn't there. The staff went through all the motions of feeding the dog and the drunk's eyes got wider and wider and finally he dropped the dog's chain and fled into the night. 'How is the dog?' Harry asked the next time the man came in. 'I'm cured' was the answer."[13]

Women at Harry's Bar

After WWII, Harry distributed a small 100-page booklet entitled *What I Know About Women*, whose pages were completely blank!

Yet female customers have always frequented Harry's Bar, and unlike some establishments where, even until recently, unaccompanied ladies were kindly requested to leave, they have never felt a moment's unease at Harry's – quite the contrary.

For the ladies too, the bar in Rue Daunou was also a "Little America", with its relaxed atmosphere and where, during the Roaring Twenties, the mix of jazz, cocktails and Americans allowed people to have a good time without incurring the cost of a sea voyage to the United States!

Today, Harry's gets its fair share of women patrons, unaccompanied or not, who often prefer the cozier ambience of the piano-bar. They also like to frequent it at lunch times[14] or in the afternoon, when it's quieter.

Fashion models are also frequent visitors and have their favorite barmen, never missing the opportunity to stop by to say hello during Paris Fashion Week. Fashion magazines have often used the décor for their photo shoots and the women who work for jewelers, banks and legal practices in and around Place Vendôme also rapidly become regulars. Perhaps inspired by Isabelle MacElhone, the current *patronne*, Harry's reserves a particularly attentive welcome for its female patrons.

13. *The Ocean Press*, 1949

14. In addition to its legendary *chiens chauds*, Harry's Bar now serves a light menu at lunchtime – the only time when you can order, and be served, coffee!

AU HARRY'S BAR

Ungaro – Robe en crêpe de laine noir de Lan-be imprimé de fleurs multicolores d'après un dessin de Sonia Knapp. Buste long et jupe à plis. Col noué en voile de laine blanc. Jean-Louis Scherrer – Dans une harmonie de rouge, gris et brun, une robe chemisier et un deux pièces en crêpe de laine imprimée de Staron. La veste de l'ensemble décolletée ras du cou est resserrée à la taille par une ceinture coulissée.

CLAUS OHM

148

GUINNESS
IS GOOD FOR YOU

1. Marken-Cocktailrührer, Harry's Bar Genf / Branded cocktail stirrer, Harry's Bar, Geneva.
2. In Harry's Bar in München / Inside Harry's Bar in Munich
3. Außenansicht von Harry's Bar in Montreux / *The front of Harry's Bar, Montreux*

1.

HARRY'S BAR **AROUND** THE **WORLD**

HARRY'S BAR IN ALLER **WELT**

Bereits 1931 bot Harry MacElhone, der auf vielen Gebieten ein Pionier war, einem italienschen Freund ein »Franchise« an. Der Mann, der in einem Hotel in Venedig als Concierge arbeitete, hatte gerade ein wenig Geld geerbt und spielte mit dem Gedanken, eine Trattoria aufzumachen. Doch Harry schlug vor, damit eine Filiale von Harry's Bar in Venedig zu eröffnen. Am Ende wurde die Vereinbarung zwischen den beiden Gentlemen nicht in die Tat umgesetzt, da sich die Zeiten und die beteiligten Personen geändert hatten. Immerhin wurden in Paris weiterhin Cocktails gerührt und gemixt und keine Pasta.

Andernorts aber entstanden Filialen von Harry's Bar, stets unter Aufsicht des Pariser Originaletablissements. Dabei wird sehr auf den Schutz der Marken, Logos und des Ambientes geachtet. In den Fünfzigerjahren wurde eine Filiale in Florenz eröffnet. 1974 war München an der Reihe, wo die Pariser Bar genau nachgebaut wurde und schnell zum angesagten Treff der Stadt avancierte. Ihre Weihe erhielt sie von IBF-Mitgliedern wie Helmut Schmidt, die sie zu ihrer »Trap« (Falle) machten. In München wurden auch Biertrink-Wettbewerbe und Straw Votee veranstaltet. Harrys Enkel, Duncan MacElhone, eröffnete 1984 eine Filiale in Montreux. Berlin zog 1988 mit einer Filiale im Esplanade Hotel nach, Hannover 1995 mit einer solchen im Pelikan Hotel, Frankfurt folgte 2001 und Köln 2003 mit einer Filiale im Intercontinental.

Die Gäste bleiben Harry's stets treu und freuen sich, dass sie überall die einzigartige Atmosphäre der Originalbar genießen können und ebenso die erstklassigen Cocktails, auf die sich der Ruf der Bar stützt. Es gibt viele Anfragen für ein Franchise, aber der Auswahlprozess ist hart. Zu viel steht auf dem Spiel, wenn man immer mehr Bars mit diesem Markennamen aufmacht, damit nicht am Ende der Geist des Originals auf der Strecke bleibt.

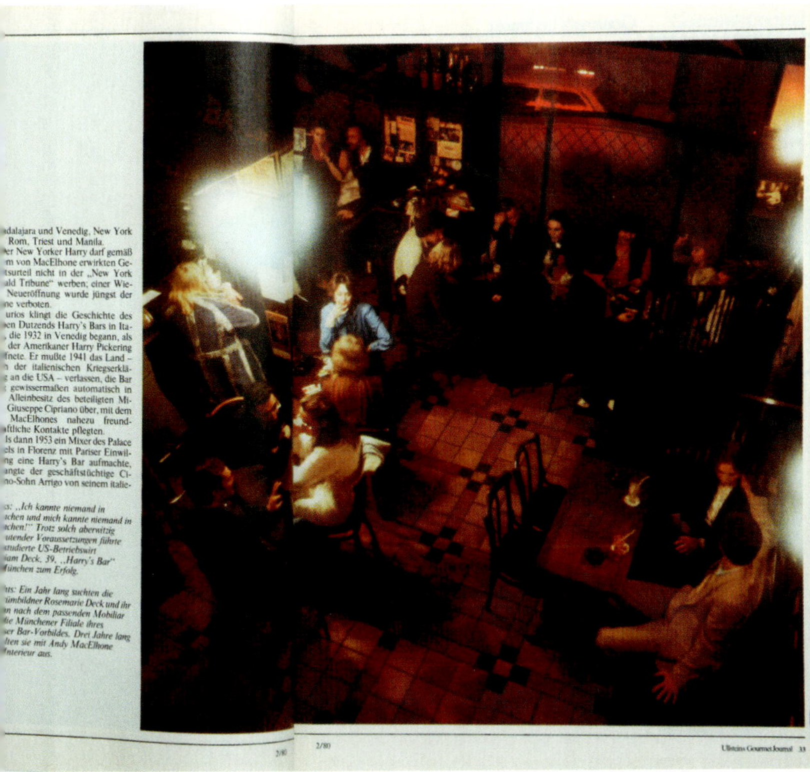
adalajara und Venedig, New York
Rom, Triest und Manila.
er New Yorker Harry darf gemäß
m von MacElhone erwirkten Ge-
tsurteil nicht in der „New York
ald Tribune" werben; einer Wie-
Neueröffnung wurde jüngst der
ne verboten.
urios klingt die Geschichte des
en Dutzends Harry's Bars in Ita-
, die 1932 in Venedig begann, als
der Amerikaner Harry Pickering
fnete. Er mußte 1941 das Land –
n der italienischen Kriegserklä-
g an die USA – verlassen, die Bar
gewissermaßen automatisch in
Alleinbesitz des beteiligten Mi-
Giuseppe Cipriano über, mit dem
MacElhones nahezu freund-
ftliche Kontakte pflegten.
ls dann 1953 ein Mixer des Palace
els in Florenz mit Pariser Einwil-
ng eine Harry's Bar aufmachte,
angte der geschäftstüchtige Ci-
no-Sohn Arrigo von seinem italie-

s: „Ich kannte niemand in
chen und mich kannte niemand in
chen!" Trotz solch aberwitzig
utender Voraussetzungen führte
studierte US-Betriebswirt
iam Deck, 39, „Harry's Bar"
München zum Erfolg.

ts: Ein Jahr lang suchten die
ümbildner Rosemarie Deck und ihr
n nach dem passenden Mobiliar
die Münchener Filiale ihres
ser Bar-Vorbildes. Drei Jahre lang
lten sie mit Andy MacElhone
Interieur aus.

2.

UN BAR AMÉRICAIN CRÉÉ À MONTREUX

3.

Clearly a pioneer in many a field, as early as 1931, Harry MacElhone granted a "franchise" to an Italian friend who had just come into a small inheritance, and who had initially considered opening a trattoria in Venice. The Italian, who was at that time a concierge in a Venice hotel, was offered the opportunity to open up a "Harry's Bar" in that city. The gentlemen's agreement between these two real gentlemen eventually lapsed as the times and the people involved changed. In Paris, however, cocktails (not pasta) continued to be shaken and stirred.

Several other incarnations of Harry's Bar blossomed in other countries, under the supervision and control of the original. Harry's is protective of the trademarks, the logos and the ambiance. In the 1950s a Harry's Bar opened in Florence. In 1974, it was the turn of Munich, where a virtual replica of the Paris bar quickly became the city's "It" place and was consecrated by members of the I.B.F. (including Helmut Schmidt), who made it one of their "traps". It also featured the beer drinking contests and Straw votes. A call even went out to try and coin the phonetic German equivalent of *Sank Roo Doe Noo*, but no proposal proved fully satisfactory. Duncan MacElhone, Harry's grandson, opened a Harry's Bar in Montreux in 1984. Berlin followed suit in 1988 at the Esplanade Hotel, Hanover in 1995 at the Pelikan Hotel, Frankfurt in 2001 and Cologne in 2003 at the Intercontinental.

Customers are always loyal to the cause, happy to find the same warm, unique atmosphere of the original, and the cocktails on which its reputation is built. There have been many franchise applications, but the selection process is draconian. There is too much to lose by increasing the number of branded venues if the spirit of the original Harry's is lacking.

1. Sidecar (1931).
2. Blue Lagoon (1960).
3. Harry's Pick Me Up (1925).

THE **COCKTAIL** EMPORIUM

DAS **COCKTAIL**-ZENTRUM

1.

Harry war ein Künstler, der sich für jede Gelegenheit einen neuen Cocktail ausdachte. Er und sein Team haben eine stattliche Anzahl mit aktuellem Zeitbezug kreiert. Der *Tlevesoor Cocktail* (»Roosevelt« rückwärts gelesen) zum Beispiel wurde erstmals 1932 gemixt, als Roosevelt zum Präsidenten der Vereinigten Staaten gewählt wurde, der *Coronation 1937 Cocktail* anlässlich der Krönung König Georgs VI. von England am 12. Mai 1937. Die Liste der Klassiker, die in Harry's Bar entwickelt wurden, ist sehr lang und schließt den *Blue Lagoon* und den *Sidecar* ein. Und auch wenn einige die Urheberschaft des berühmten *Bloody Mary* für sich reklamieren, der 1921 ebenfalls in Harry's Bar von Pete Petiot[15] kreiert wurde, übersehen sie leider, dass eine solche Hommage an Mary Tudor nur einem Untertan Ihrer Allergnädigen Majestät zustand ... ebenso wie die Veredelung von amerikanischem Tomatensaft aus der Dose!

Für die Befreiung von Paris wurde in Harry's Bar kein Cocktail erfunden. Welcher Drink wäre diesem Wunder auch gerecht geworden? 1945 jedoch bot die Bar einen *UN-Cocktail* an zu Feier der Gründung der Vereinten Nationen am 25. Juni. Viele weitere zeitbezogene Kreationen folgten, auch durch Andrew MacElhone, der die Tradition weiterführte, indem er die erste Mondlandung mit dem *Moon Shot* zelebrierte, wie auch später durch Duncan MacElhone, der mit den ersten alkoholfreien Cocktails *Safe Speed* und *Long Drive* neue Wege ging. Was in einem solchen Lokal leicht als Hochverrat hätte gelten können, zeigte nur einmal mehr, dass man bei Harry's die Zeichen der Zeit zu erkennen pflegt. Der Meister der Cocktail-Kunst stellt sich der Aufgabe, auch Gäste zu begeistern, die noch fahren müssen. Diese Kreationen wurden dankend von Leuten angenommen, die ihren Führerschein behalten wollten. Und wollte ein Gast wirklich auf Nummer sicher gehen, wussten die stets wachsamen Barkeeper, wann es Zeit für eine Pause war. Was Andrew MacElhone sagte und von Antoine Blondin in *Monsieur Jardis*[16] zitiert wurde,

15. Pete Petiot verließ Paris und führte die Bar im St. Regis in New York.
16. *La Table Ronde*, 1970 und1972, Seite 36.

2.

3.

Harry was a true artist who loved to dream up a new cocktail for every grand occasion. He and his team are credited with inventing an impressive series of cocktails with a topical twist. The Tlevesoor Cocktail ("Roosevelt" written back-to-front) was first mixed for his election as president of the United States in 1932, while the Coronation 1937 Cocktail marked the crowning of the new King of England, George VI, on 12 May 1937. The list of classics created at Harry's Bar, which includes the Blue Lagoon and the Sidecar, is extremely lengthy. And although some may try to appropriate the paternity of the celebrated Bloody Mary, created in 1921 at Harry's by mixologist Pete Petiot[15], they forget that only a subject of Her Gracious Majesty was allowed to pay this "tribute" to Mary Tudor... and also to celebrate the American art of canning tomato juice!

Harry's Bar did not invent a cocktail for the Liberation of Paris, as no drink could hope to rival the wonder of the event. But in 1945, the Bar was offering a UN Cocktail to mark the creation of the United Nations Organization on 25 June. Many others followed, and the tradition was upheld by Andrew MacElhone, whose *Moon Shot* celebrated the first man on the moon, and then by Duncan MacElhone, who broke new ground by creating the alcohol-free cocktails Safe Speed and Long Drive. What might have been seen as high treason in such a venue in fact turned out to be a further illustration of Harry's knack for staying attuned to the times. The unchallenged master of the art of mixing cocktails set himself the challenge of helping customers taking the wheel to have a good time at Harry's anyway. These creations, whose evocative names say it all, have been warmly saluted by the people trying to get points put back on their driving licenses. In fact, if a patron has erred on the side of incaution, the ever-watchful barmen know when to suggest that they take a little break. Similarly, Andrew MacElhone, cited by Antoine Blondin in *Monsieur Jadis*[16], used

15. Pete Petiot subsequently left to manage the bar at the St. Regis in New York.
16. *La Table Ronde*, Paris, 1970, and *Folio*, Paris, 1972, p. 36.

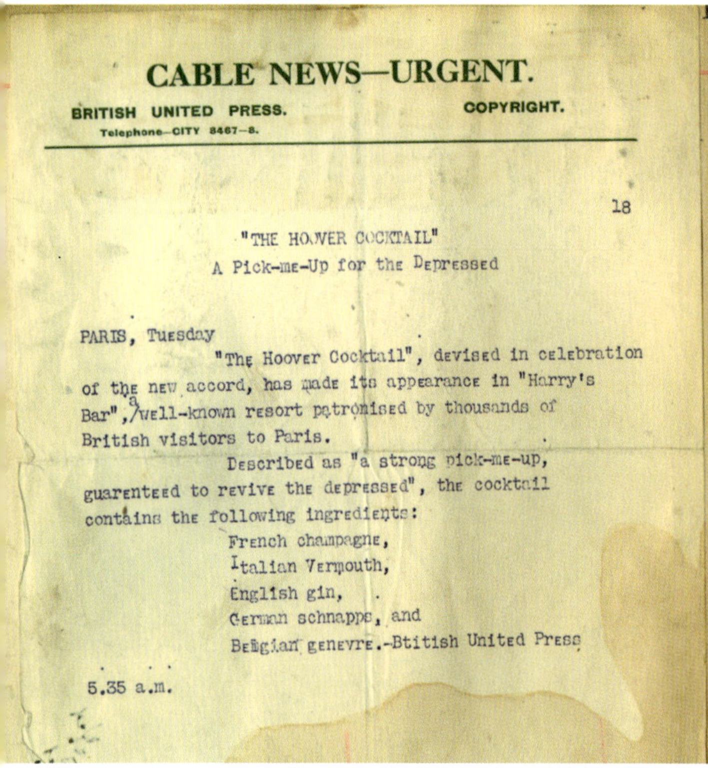

CABLE NEWS—URGENT.

BRITISH UNITED PRESS. COPYRIGHT.

Telephone—CITY 8467–8.

18

"THE HOOVER COCKTAIL"
A Pick-me-Up for the Depressed

PARIS, Tuesday

"The Hoover Cocktail", devised in celebration of the new accord, has made its appearance in "Harry's Bar", a well-known resort patronised by thousands of British visitors to Paris.

Described as "a strong pick-me-up, guarenteed to revive the depressed", the cocktail contains the following ingredients:

French champagne,
Italian Vermouth,
English gin,
German schnapps, and
Belgian genevre.-Btitish United Press

5.35 a.m.

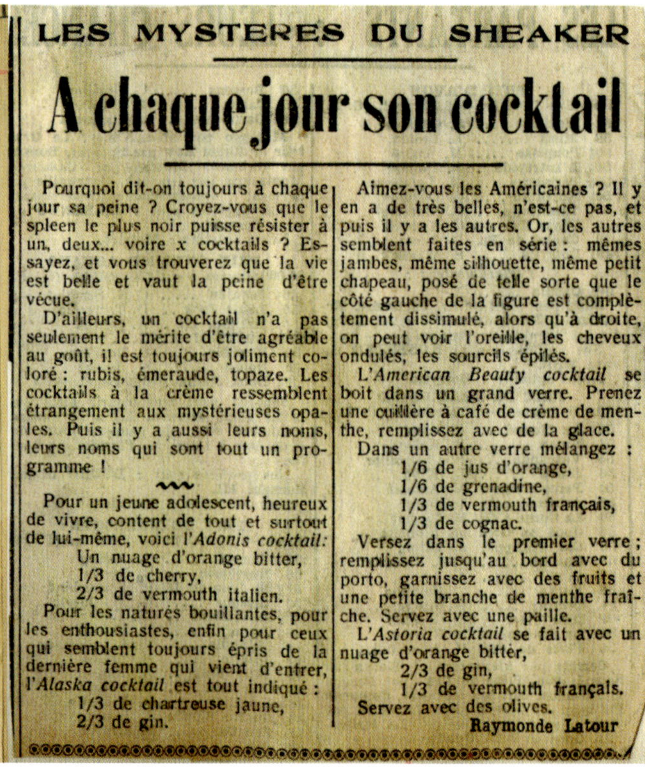

LES MYSTERES DU SHEAKER

A chaque jour son cocktail

Pourquoi dit-on toujours à chaque jour sa peine ? Croyez-vous que le spleen le plus noir puisse résister à un, deux... voire *x* cocktails ? Essayez, et vous trouverez que la vie est belle et vaut la peine d'être vécue.

D'ailleurs, un cocktail n'a pas seulement le mérite d'être agréable au goût, il est toujours joliment coloré : rubis, émeraude, topaze. Les cocktails à la crème ressemblent étrangement aux mystérieuses opales. Puis il y a aussi leurs noms, leurs noms qui sont tout un programme !

Pour un jeune adolescent, heureux de vivre, content de tout et surtout de lui-même, voici l'*Adonis cocktail:*

Un nuage d'orange bitter,
1/3 de cherry,
2/3 de vermouth italien.

Pour les natures bouillantes, pour les enthousiastes, enfin pour ceux qui semblent toujours épris de la dernière femme qui vient d'entrer, l'*Alaska cocktail* est tout indiqué :

1/3 de chartreuse jaune,
2/3 de gin.

Aimez-vous les Américaines ? Il y en a de très belles, n'est-ce pas, et puis il y a les autres. Or, les autres semblent faites en série : mêmes jambes, même silhouette, même petit chapeau, posé de telle sorte que le côté gauche de la figure est complètement dissimulé, alors qu'à droite, on peut voir l'oreille, les cheveux ondulés, les sourcils épilés.

L'*American Beauty cocktail* se boit dans un grand verre. Prenez une cuillère à café de crème de menthe, remplissez avec de la glace.

Dans un autre verre mélangez :

1/6 de jus d'orange,
1/6 de grenadine,
1/3 de vermouth français,
1/3 de cognac.

Versez dans le premier verre ; remplissez jusqu'au bord avec du porto, garnissez avec des fruits et une petite branche de menthe fraîche. Servez avec une paille.

L'*Astoria cocktail* se fait avec un nuage d'orange bitter,

2/3 de gin,
1/3 de vermouth français.

Servez avec des olives.

Raymonde Latour

geht in dieselbe Richtung: *Es ist eine seltsame französische Krankheit, Leute unter dem Vorwand der Trunkenheit rauszuwerfen. Dabei sollte man sie dann erst recht im Warmen behalten. Das ist überlebenswichtig.* Die Aufmerksamkeit, die man den Gästen angedeihen lässt, hört da aber nicht auf. Hat jemand einen Kater, egal ob bei Harry's oder andernorts entstanden, haben die Barkeeper ein Zaubermittel namens *Prairie Oyster* parat. In die Basismischung kommen Aspirin, ein Teelöffel leichtes Abführmittel, ein Dutzend Tropfen Angostura Bitter und je ein kleiner Schuss Brandy und Sherry. Anschließend wird ein frisches Ei hineingeschlagen und das Glas mit Clubsoda aufgegossen. Das Glas muss in einem Zug geleert werden. Die Heilkraft liegt im Eigelb, das man in Ganzen schluckt. Hat man den *Prairie Oyster* unten, ist der Kater bald vergessen.

In Harry's Bar achtet man darauf, dass die Cocktailliste laufend auf den neuesten Stand gebracht wird. Die Bar geht keine Kompromisse ein, wenn es um die Qualität und Dosierung der Spirituosen geht, die für ihre Cocktails, Short- und Longdrinks verwendet werden. Die großen Klassiker wurden immer dann entwickelt, wenn ein neuer Likör, Schnaps oder eine neue Zutat auf den Markt kam. Der *Bloody Mary* zum Beispiel entstand, als Tomatensaft in Dosen aufkam. Der *Blue Lagoon* ist das Ergebnis einer Falschlieferung von Curaçao mit einer merkwürdigen blauen Farbe, den Andrew MacElhone als sparsamer Schotte lieber für Cocktails verwendete, als ihn wegzuschütten. Einen künftigen Klassiker zu kreieren ist jedoch nicht einfach. Oft wird hastig etwas zusammengemischt, das im Ergebnis unbefriedigend ist und dennoch als kreativ verkauft wird.

Solche Drinks sind in Harry's Bar verboten, dessen Team aus erstklassigen Barkeepern die Worte von Duncan MacElhone verinnerlicht hat: *An den Klassikern pfuscht man nicht herum. Sie sind unveränderlich und werden die Zeiten überdauern.* Der große Klassiker in Harry's Bar ist zweifellos der *Bloody Mary*, von dem 2010 über 9000 Gläser serviert wurden, dicht gefolgt vom *Mojito*, der einen Großteil seines Ruhms Ernest Hemingway und dessen zahlreichen Reisen nach Kuba verdankt. Dahinter kommen der *Piña Colada* mit 2100 und schließlich der *Manhattan* mit über 1000 Bestellungen. Cocktails gibt es in zahllosen Varianten, und jeder hat seinen ganz eigenen Charakter, auch wenn die Spezialisten bei Harry's aus praktisch allen Zutaten Cocktail-Begeisterung entfachen können.

to say, "It's a curious French malady to throw people out on the pretext that they are drunk. On the contrary, you should keep them in the warmth. It's elementary." But the little attentions for customers don't stop there. Should a customer have a hangover, whether or not due to the liquid fare served at Harry's, the barmen have a magic cure-all called the Prairie Oyster, a mix based on aspirin, a teaspoonful of a mild purgative, a dozen drops of Angostura bitters, a small measure of brandy and one of sherry. A fresh egg is then added into the mixture and the glass is topped with a little club soda. It must be downed in one gulp: the cure comes from swallowing the yolk without breaking it. Having downed the Prairie Oyster, the drinker's hangover is very soon no more than a distant bad memory!

Harry's Bar has always paid great attention to its cocktail list, which is constantly updated, and the Bar is uncompromising when it comes to the quality and dosage of the spirits used for its cocktails and short and long drinks. The great classics were invented over the years, when a new liqueur, spirit or ingredient came on the market. The Bloody Mary, for example, was born at the same time as canned tomato juice appeared. The Blue Lagoon is the outcome of a "failed" delivery of bottles of curaçao with an odd blue color, which Andrew MacElhone, a true thrifty Scot, preferred to use in a cocktail rather than pour down the drain. But it isn't easy to create a cocktail that's destined to become a classic. Mixes can often be rash, if not downright ridiculous, and the customers in some establishments may easily become unwitting guinea pigs for doubtful elixirs where appearance and supposed creativity are considered more important than harmonious taste.

Such drinks are banned from Harry's Bar, whose team of top mixologists, constantly remember what Duncan MacElhone drilled into them: "You don't meddle with the classics. They are unchanging and stand the test of time." So while the great classic at Harry's Bar is undoubtedly the Bloody Mary (more than 9,000 prepared in 2010), close on its heels comes the Mojito, whose fame owes a great deal to Ernest Hemingway's many trips to Cuba, and, following closely behind, the 2,100 Piña Coladas and more than 1,000 Manhattans served there. There are cocktails, and then there are cocktails, each one with its own unique character, even if the mixologists at Harry's can mix up a storm with any ingredients!

1. Das Barkeeper-Team in Harry's Bar, mit Franz-Arthur, Harry MacElhones Urenkel (Mitte) / *The team of barmen at Harry's Bar, with Franz-Arthur, great-grandson of Harry MacElhone (center).*

HARRY'S BAR **YESTERDAY,** TODAY, **TOMORROW**

HARRY'S BAR **GESTERN,** HEUTE **MORGEN**

Harry's Bar ist nicht nur eine Institution oder ein Ort, an dem man als junger Mensch Abende verbracht hat, an die man sich lange erinnert. Sie ist viel mehr. Und ihr bis heute anhaltender Erfolg auch bei einer jungen, anspruchsvollen Klientel ist der Lohn für die ungebrochene Authentizität eines Etablissments, das sich dem Wandel des Zeitgeists nicht verschlossen und dennoch seine Seele bewahrt hat. Der Zauber beginnt zu wirken, sobald man die Flügeltüren aufstößt. Welches Geheimnis steckt hinter der Langlebigkeit dieser Bar? Vielleicht, dass Harry's so gar nichts mit den trendigen Bars und In-Lokalen gemein hat, die genauso schnell verschwinden, wie sie aufmachen.

Der IBF, diese noble und respektable Institution, hat heute nicht weniger als 100 000 Mitglieder und rund 120 Traps auf fünf Kontinenten.

Viele Trittbrettfahrer haben sich widerrechtlich des Namens »Harry's Bar« bemächtigt, weil sie hoffen, dass so etwas vom Ruhm des Originals auf sie abfärbt. Harry's hat beschlossen, sich nicht an Auseinandersetzungen über die Urheberschaft bestimmter Cocktails zu beteiligen. Es gibt immer Streitereien darüber, wie eine Sage zustande kam, und am Ende profitiert nur die Sage selbst davon. Die Vielzahl an Geschichten weckt Zweifel an der Echtheit einer jeden einzelnen. Doch alle Mythen stärken letztlich nur die Legende von Harry's Bar. Und die Fakten untermauern ihren Ruhm.

Es ist noch immer die Familie MacElhone, die diese legendäre Bar betreibt. Franz-Arthur, Harry's Urenkel, wurde genau wie er am 16. Juni geboren, nur 98 Jahre später. Harry's Bar verändert sich laufend und veranstaltet in der Pianobar regelmäßig Happenings, die viel Begeisterung hervorrufen. Dennoch heißt die Bar ihre Gäste mit derselben Aufmerksamkeit wie eh und je willkommen und führt Neulinge mit Freuden in ihre Genüsse ein.

Wer kann schon voraussagen, welche Cocktails in hundert Jahren die Beliebtheitsskala anführen? Niemand natürlich. Eines aber ist gewiss: Man wird sie in Harry's Bar trinken.

Paris, September 2011

1.

Harry's Bar is not just an institution or a place where you remember spending lengthy, memorable evenings in your youth. It's much more than that, and its continuing success today with a young and exacting clientele rewards the authentic vibe of a venue that has kept its soul intact at the same time as it has changed with the times. The magic starts to work as soon as you push through the batwings. What's the secret of its longevity? Perhaps it's because Harry's is quite unlike those fashionable spots and modish bars that vanish almost as soon as they open.

The I.B.F., that noble and respectable institution, today has no fewer than 100,000 members and 120 traps on five continents.

Many copycat bars usurp the name of Harry's Bar to try and garner a bit of its fame. Harry's has decided not to enter into disputes concerning the paternity of certain cocktails. Every legend is subject to this type of appropriation and, at the end of the day, so much the better for the legend! The multiplicity of stories makes their authenticity doubtful, but all the myths only serve to strengthen the legend of Harry's Bar. The facts are there to underpin its fame, and that is partly the raison d'être of this modest work, which, we hope, will also have entertained you.

The MacElhone family, for its part, is still at the helm of this legendary bar. Franz-Arthur, Harry's great-grandson, was born, like him, on a 16 June, ninety-eight years down the line! Harry's Bar is changing, and regularly organizes happenings in the piano-bar that generate plenty of buzz. It still welcomes its patrons with the same attentiveness, as it strives to initiate newcomers into its pleasures.

Who can predict which cocktails will be most popular a hundred years hence? No-one, of course. But what we *can* be sure of, is that they will be drinking them in Harry's Bar.

Paris, September 2011

74. DIE **ÄLTESTE** COCKTAILBAR **IN EUROPA**

ARE YOU AN I.B.F.
ARMY
Maker's Mark

Harry's New-York Bar

WHITE LADY

- $^{1}/_{3}$ Zitronensaft
- $^{1}/_{3}$ weißer Pfefferminzlikör
- $^{1}/_{3}$ Cointreau

Gut schütteln und abseihen.

Das war das Originalrezept, das Harry MacElhone 1919 im Ciro's Club in London entwickelt hatte.

1929 in Harry's Bar in Paris änderte er es folgendermaßen ab:

- $^{1}/_{3}$ Gin
- $^{1}/_{3}$ Cointreau
- $^{1}/_{3}$ Zitronensaft

Harry als Chefbarkeeper im Ciro's in London.

Das Ciro's in Deauville

78. **26.** NOVEMBER **1911**

Eröffnung

1923

1925

1933

Dimanche 26 Novembre 1911
CINQ CENTIMES

Le Petit Parisien
Supplément Littéraire Illustré

PIERRE Ier, ROI DE SERBIE

Vin Extra 28 cent. le litre. Échant.ons Gratis ROUX, à FONS (Gard)

CYCLES MERICANT 13, Av. des Moulineaux, PARIS-BILLANCOURT Catalogue franco. PRIX de GROS aux Intermédiaires

Le Gérant: BOUQUET.

Paris. — BOUQUET, imprimeur du Petit Parisien, 18, rue d'Enghien.

RIRE s'amuser, amuser la société, demander les 3 catalog. Farces, Attrapes, Chansons, Physique, Magie, Magnétisme, Hypnotisme, etc. Gratis. BAUDOT, 3, Rue des Carmes, Paris. MAISON FONDÉE EN 1800.

POMMADE MOULIN
Guérit Dartres, Boutons, Rougeurs, Démangeaisons, Eczéma, Hémorroïdes. Fait repousser les Cheveux et les Cils. Le Pt 2/50 franco Phie Moulin 30, Rue Louis-le-Grand, PARIS

SITUATION D'AVENIR

Reproduced with kind permission of MR. L. Saalburg and Esquire Magazine

SANK ROO DOE NOO PARIS

1939

1980

1992

SINGER

MLLE. JANYL, who sings nightly at Harry's New York Bar, accompanied by Roy Barton.

AMERICAN BAR.

"HARRY'S" New York Bar

(Opposite Ciro's) 6 RUE DAUNOU

KEL KEECH — CABARET — LEO DESLYS

SMARTEST BOHEMIAN PLACE IN TOWN

LÉO DESLYS AND ROY BARTON

American Singers of Class, now entertaining at

HARRY'S NEW YORK BAR

5, RUE DAUNOU

The "Jumping-Off Place"

HARRYS New-York Bar

5, Rue Daunou, 5 PARIS

The "JUMPING-OFF PLACE'

Come and kill time during those dull hours between dinner and dance time

ROY, BARTON and LEO DESLY'S

In their latest compositions "After The Rain," "Shanghai Poppy-Man" and "Montmartre Rose"

"HARRY'S" NEW YORK BAR

5 RUe Daunou (off Rue de la Paix), PARIS

HARRY PRESENTS...
His new cabaret
downstairs

"THE FRONT PAGE"

and hopes you will drop in at
5, RUE DAUNOU

any time between the hours of
5 P. M. to 8 P. M.

SATURDAY 20th MAY

HARRY PRESENTE
son nouveau cabaret
au sous-sol

"LA PREMIÈRE PAGE"

et attend votre visite
5, RUE DAUNOU

à n'importe quel moment, entre
17 et 20 heures

SAMEDI 20 MAI

FRONT PAGE CABARET

DOWNSTAIRS EVERY EVENIN

THE DOWNSTAIRS CABARET
HARRY'S NEW YORK BAR (IBF) Headquarters) 5, RUE DAUNOU, PARIS
SUMMER SEASON HARRY'S BAR — LE TOUQUET

Harry's New-York Bar

CHAMPAGNERCOCKTAIL

Im Weinglas:

- 1 mit Angostura getränkter Zuckerwürfel
- 5 Spritzer Cognac
- Eis

Mit Champagner auffüllen und eine Zitronenschale darüber ausdrücken.

DER **NACHTCLUB** IM KELLER

HARRY'S NEW-YORK BAR
5, Rue Daunou
Paris-Opéra district
JUST TELL THE TAXI DRIVER
"SANK ROO DOE NOO"
BAR OPEN ALL DAY AND NIGHT
TÉL. OPÉRA 73-00
Offert gracieusement
par HARRY'S NEW-YORK BAR - Paris
CONCESSIONNAIRE DE LA PUBLICITE SUR CES POCHETTES
TELEPHONE ELY. 60-16 LASTAR 6R. LINCOLN PARIS (8e)
WITH COMPLIMENTS OF BOB, CHARLIE AND JACK
HARRY'S NEW-YORK BAR
5 RUE DAUNOU
PARIS
1951 BIMILLÉNAIRE DE BIMILLENARY OF PARIS
HARRY'S NEW-YORK BAR
5, Rue Daunou - PARIS
Le
de
l'Exposition
se trouve au
HARRY'S-BAR
5, RUE DAUNOU — PARIS (près l'Opéra)
Tous les Soirs, CABARET
York Bar
PURGE BÉBÉ
POUR LES VOIES URINAIRES CONSULTEZ LE DOCTEUR CALIGARI
SI-VOUS-AVEZ LE SOUVENIR D'AMOUR
DR. CUREM AWL PILULES
THE JUMPING-OFF PLACE
ROY BARTON AND LEO DESLYS
SING EVERY EVENING
MALADE
WHEN I'M
FULL
TAKE ME HOME
RING THE BELL
WISH ME WELL
RUN LIKE HELL
Contre
les
Bonimenteurs
et
Pessimistes
HARRY'S NEW-YORK BAR
I. B. F.
Headquarters. Trap No I
5, Rue Daunou — PARIS
TEL.: OPE. 73-00
Just Tell The Taxi Driver "Sank Roo Doe Noo"
Address where I am staying
LA DIRECTION VOUS PRIE
DE QUITTER CET ÉTABLISSEMENT
ET DE NE PLUS Y REVENIR.
H. N. Y. B. - PARIS
THIS MEANS "SCRAM"

WONDER WHY FOLKS WORRY?

There are only two reasons for worry, you are either successful or you are not successful. If you are successful there is nothing to worry about; if you are not successful there are only two things to worry about. Your health is either good or you are sick. If your health is good there is nothing to worry about; if you are sick there are again only two things to worry about. You are either going to get well or you are going to die. If you are going to get well there is nothing to worry about; if you are going to die there are again only two things to worry about. You are either going to Heaven or you are going to Hell. If you are going to Heaven there is nothing to worry about; if you are going to Hell, you will be so jolly busy shaking hands with your old friends that you won't have time to worry at all.

SO WHY WORRY?

Come to

HARRY'S NEW YORK BAR

Sank Roo Doe Noo Paris

The Next BARFLY who comes weeping to you cr "BAD BUSINESS" hand him this CRYING TOWEL — d him to a quiet corner and tell him the advantag

Boosting Business

Prosperity is round the corner "yeah"

Which corner?

Harry's New-York Bar

HARRY'S PICK ME UP

- 2 Spritzer Grenadine
- Saft einer ½ Zitrone
- 2 Unzen (60 ml) Cognac

Gut schütteln und in ein mittelgroßes Glas abseihen, mit Champagner auffüllen.

(1925 in Harry's Bar von Harry MacElhone erfunden.)

What I Know About Women

by

HARRY Mc ELHONE

HARRY'S NEW YORK BAR PARIS

(through whose doors pass the most lovely Women of the World)

TELL THE TAXI DRIVER

Sank roo doe noo

Bar open all Day and Night

Cabaret every evening

Tel.: OPE. 73-00

"HERES HOW

he horse and cow live thirty years
hey touch light wines and beers.
eep and goats are dead at twenty,
hey drink no liquor water plenty.
ten the cat has lost nine lives.
n milk and water no man thrives.
five the birds are mostly dead.
hey look not on the wine thats red.
ngs few days remain on earth.
hey do not know cocktails worth.
ut sinful ginful rum soaked men,
ive on for three score years and ten.

Bull and Gasbag rotector

SERVIETTE POUR PERSONNE QUI PLEURE

(DE PLUS EN PLUS EN VOGUE)

BE "SEEIN YA"

at cocktail time

MAC" and "ANDY"

VILL MIX YOU THE BEST

ET EVERY NITE

9 P.M. TILL 2. A M

S NEW-YORK BAR

UNOU PARIS — TEL. OPERA 73-00

Am 26. Juni 1932 trinkt der Amerikaner Henry Cochran zwei Liter Bier in elf Sekunden.

Present Record
2 Liters: 11 Sec
2 Quarts 1/10 : 11 Sec

TRYING TO BREAK THE 11 SECOND TWO LITRES BEER DRINKING RECORD AT HARRY'S NEW YORK BAR L.B.F. TRAP N° 1 PARIS

Any challenger failing to beat the record will be charge[d] for the beer.

Time	Date	Name	Home Town	Witnesses
19 Seconds	August 5th 1925	Charlie Spahn	New York	G. Ambler G. A. Trost
8½ "	aug -- 14th 1926	Phil Fowler Dartmouth	Boston - Mas	TIME KEEPER: Harry H. G. Hill T. H. Wilson
7 "	aug -- 2nd 1923	Jack Frost (Harvard)	Cleveland - Ohio	TIMEKEEPER: Harry T. C. Ayres, Her Hyman
7 "	July 21st - 1931	Allan Watkins	Atlanta - Georgia	TIMEKEEPER: Harry R. Mackie H. Jendins, W. M
3 "	June 6th - 1932	Jack Robbins	Bridgeport - Penn	TIMEKEEPER Harry Webb Miller. W. Jennings, M M
1 "	June 26th 1932	J. Henri Cochran (Princeton)	Williamsport. Penn	TIMEKEEPER Harry. S. Bull, R. Bartlett WM S Sam Helman. Marcel Achard

Biertrink-Wettbewerb in Harry's Bar in Le Touquet.

Giving 'Em the Boot in France

VETSPORT AND CHILI-CON-CARNE PARTY

Given by Benjamin Franklin Post No. 605 V. F. W., September 20, 1930. Comrade John J. McGrath who holds the world's 2-liter beer-drinking record of 17½ seconds, taking a flyer at the 3-liter bootful. The timer is "Harry" of Harry's New York Bar, Paris. Our thanks to Charles H. Weigandt, Editor of "The Gold Striper," for this foto, taken during the festivities at the

WHAT A KICK IN THIS BOOT!

BEER-DRINKING CONTEST IS GREAT EVENT AT THE VETERANS OF FOREIGN WARS' SPORTS DAY!

ASSOCIATED PRESS PHOTO SHOWS JIMMY KING, OF NEW YORK, TRYING TO BEAT THE WORLDS RECORD FOR BEER DRINKING AT THE SPORTS DAY OF THE VETERANS OF FOREIGN WARS IN PARIS AT THE PARIS POLICE SPORTS GROUND. HOLDING WATCH IS HARRY McELHONE, FAMOUS HEAD OF "HARRY'S BAR" IN PARIS.

PAR-GILL 26532

Home of the "International Bar Fly"
BUZZZZ
ZZ
BUZZZZ
18€
Now or Never!
Let's try the
GLENMORANGIE
MADEIRA wood Finish
Absinthe
15,00€
Cucumber Syrup
Absinthe "Pernod"
COLUMBIA

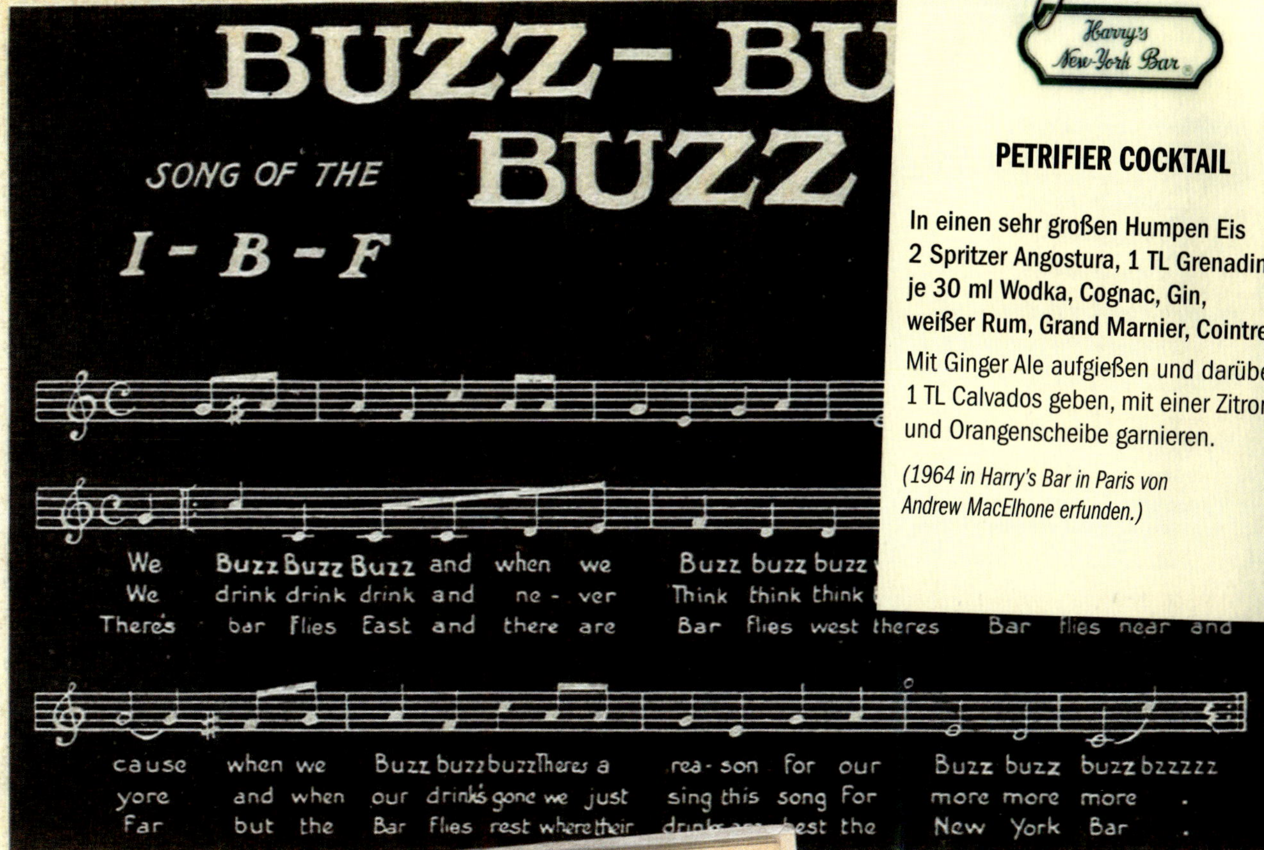

Harry's New-York Bar

PETRIFIER COCKTAIL

In einen sehr großen Humpen Eis
2 Spritzer Angostura, 1 TL Grenadine,
je 30 ml Wodka, Cognac, Gin,
weißer Rum, Grand Marnier, Cointreau.

Mit Ginger Ale aufgießen und darüber 1 TL Calvados geben, mit einer Zitronen- und Orangenscheibe garnieren.

(1964 in Harry's Bar in Paris von Andrew MacElhone erfunden.)

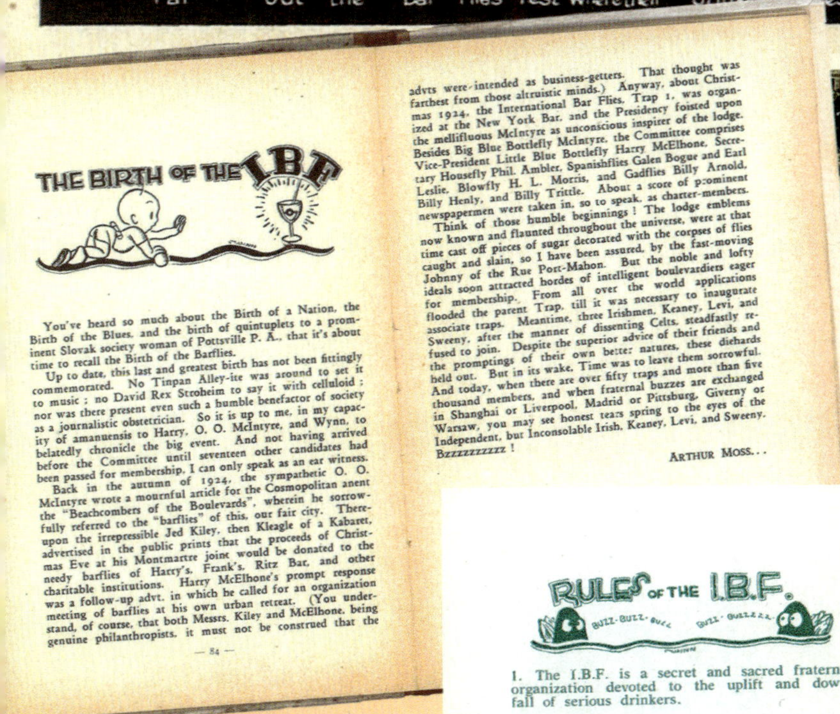

THE BIRTH OF THE I.B.F

You've heard so much about the Birth of a Nation, the Birth of the Blues, and the birth of quintuplets to a prom- inent Slovak society woman of Pottsville P. A., that it's about time to recall the Birth of the Barflies.

Up to date, this last and greatest birth has not been fittingly commemorated. No Tinpan Alley-ite was around to set it to music ; no David Rex Stroheim to say it with celluloid ; nor was there present even such a humble benefactor of society as a journalistic obstetrician. So it is up to me, in my capac- ity of amanuensis to Harry, O. O. McIntyre, and Wynn, to belatedly chronicle the big event. And not having arrived before the Committee until seventeen other candidates had been passed for membership, I can only speak as an ear witness.

Back in the autumn of 1924, the sympathetic O. O. McIntyre wrote a mournful article for the Cosmopolitan anent the "Beachcombers of the Boulevards", wherein he sorrow- fully referred to the "barflies" of this, our fair city. There- upon the irrepressible Jed Kiley, then Kleagle of a Kabaret, advertised in the public prints that the proceeds of Christ- mas Eve at his Montmartre joint would be donated to the needy barflies of Harry's, Frank's, Ritz Bar, and other charitable institutions. Harry McElhone's prompt response was a follow-up advt. in which he called for an organization meeting of barflies at his own urban retreat. (You under- stand, of course, that both Messrs. Kiley and McElhone, being genuine philanthropists, it must not be construed that the advts were intended as business-getters. That thought was farthest from those altruistic minds.) Anyway, about Christ- mas 1924, the International Bar Flies, Trap 1, was organ- ized at the New York Bar, and the Presidency foisted upon the mellifluous McIntyre as unconscious inspirer of the lodge. Besides Big Blue Bottlefly McIntyre, the Committee comprises Vice-President Little Blue Bottlefly Harry McElhone, Secre- tary Housefly Phil. Ambler, Spanishflies Galen Bogue and Earl Leslie, Blowfly H. L. Morris, and Gadflies Billy Arnold, Billy Henly, and Billy Trittle. About a score of prominent newspapermen were taken in, so to speak, as charter-members.

Think of those humble beginnings ! The lodge emblems now known and flaunted throughout the universe, were at that time cast off pieces of sugar decorated with the corpses of flies caught and slain, so I have been assured, by the fast-moving Johnny of the Rue Port-Mahon. But the noble and lofty ideals soon attracted hordes of intelligent boulevardiers eager for membership. From all over the world applications flooded the parent Trap, till it was necessary to inaugurate associate traps. Meantime, three Irishmen, Keaney, Levi, and Sweeny, after the manner of dissenting Celts, steadfastly re- fused to join. Despite the superior advice of their friends and the promptings of their own better natures, these diehards held out. But in its wake, Time was to leave them sorrowful. And today, when there are over fifty traps and more than five thousand members, and when fraternal buzzes are exchanged in Shanghai or Liverpool, Madrid or Pittsburg, Giverny or Warsaw, you may see honest tears spring to the eyes of the Independent, but Inconsolable Irish, Keaney, Levi, and Sweeny. Bzzzzzzzzz !

ARTHUR MOSS...

— 84 —

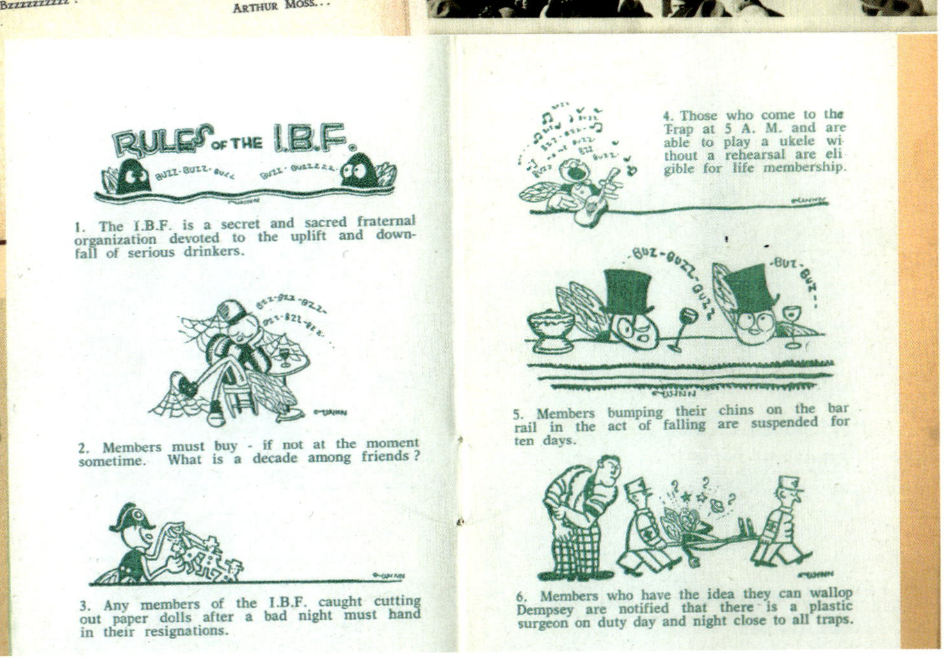

Harry's New-York Bar

OLD PAL COCKTAIL

- $^1/_3$ Canadian Whiskey
- $^1/_3$ trockener Wermut
- $^1/_3$ Campari

Rühren und servieren.

(Rezept: Sparrow Robertson, Sportredakteur der New York Herald Tribune, Paris, 1929)

88. **WHO'S** WHO **IN HARRY'S** BAR

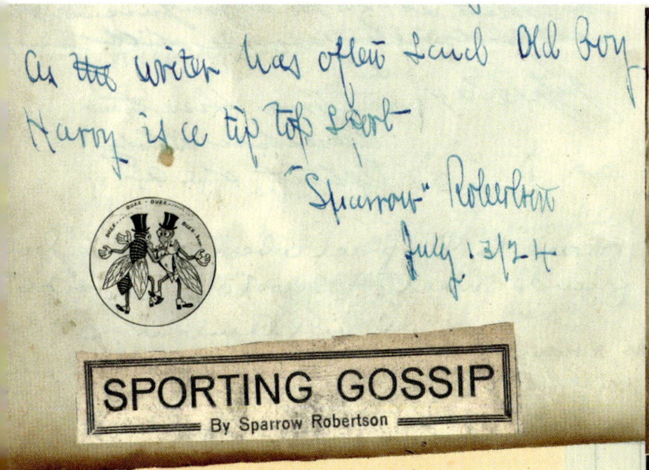

WILLIAM HARRISON (SPARROW) ROBERTSON

Sparrow Robertson wurde 1859 in Edinburgh geboren, bekam aber schon früh in seiner Karriere die amerikanische Staatsbürgerschaft. Er nannte jeden gleich »Kumpel«, egal wie kurz er ihn kannte, wofür er gleichermaßen berühmt war wie für seinen Spitznamen »Sparrow« (Spatz), der auf seine kleine Statur anspielte. In den Jahren zwischen den Weltkriegen wurde Sparrow einer der bekanntesten amerikanischen Sportjournalisten in Paris. Nachdem es ihn Ende des Ersten Weltkriegs in die französische Hauptstadt verschlagen hatte, fing er bald bei der Pariser Ausgabe der *New York Herald Tribune* an und schrieb dort zwei Jahrzehnte lang seine Sportklatschkolumne. Er sagte immer, dass er mehr amerikanische Touristen in Frankreich getroffen habe als die Visa-Abteilung der US-Botschaft. Außerdem freundete er sich mit praktisch jedem einflussreichen amerikanischen Politiker an. Er kannte auch alle Top-Athleten jener Zeit. Seine Schreibe war einzigartig, wenn sie auch manchmal jede Syntax vermissen ließ, was vermutlich daran lag, dass er die ganze Nacht die Bars durchkämmte. Am häufigsten war er in Harry's Bar zu finden, von wo aus er seine Texte telegrafierte, manchmal erst in den frühen Morgenstunden. Keiner sah ihn je ins Bett gehen ... oder seine Drinks bezahlen. Er starb am 8. Juni 1941 im Alter von 82 Jahren in seinem Haus in der Nähe von Fontainebleau.

Die »Coca-Cola Kids«.

Pour Harry
du New York Bar
qui aime Bartissol
comme moi
Marcel
STUDIO

CERDAN CHAMPION DU MONDE

près les quelques heures d'anxiété et la période d'enervement qui avaient précédé ce fameux
Cerdan - Zale, la nouvelle que notre Marcel national avait mis K.O. son adversaire et rem-
insi le titre de Champion du Monde dont la gloire rejaillissait sur la France entière fut accueil-
tous avec une explosion de joie délirante et déjà, résultat à peine connu, chacun songeait com-
élébrer dignement cette belle victoire française. Dans notre corporation ce fut une double vic-
r Marcel est en même temps le champion de « Bartissol » et cela devait se fêter comme il
nt selon le mot spirituel de notre ami Pierre Bourut, Agent général de « Bartissol » : nous
s Champions du Monde !
Il est acquis une fois pour toutes que les victoires américaines ou françaises remportées e
ique ont leur répercussion au « Harry's New-York Bar » qui est non seulement le plus vieux ba
encore le plus typiquement américain de notre capitale et son propriétaire, Harry Mac Elhone,
e figure bien parisienne malgré son accent pittoresque dont il n'a jamais pu se défaire, et sans
l d'ailleurs il ne serait plus Harry lui-même, il est Français de cœur, ne perdant jamais une
ion de montrer son contentement d'un événement heureux touchant sa seconde patrie « la
e ». C'est ainsi que le match était à peine fini qu'il téléphonait à Pierre Bourut, lequel avait
té toute la nuit la retransmission du match tressautant de joie à chaque « direct » bien sonné
de Marcel, et lui offrai
spontanément le cadr
du « Harry's New-Yor
Bar » pour célébrer ce
te victoire nationale pa
un « Cerdan Cocktail
que son fils Mac av
lui-même composé, t
lement il était sûr
Marcel. Toute la jo
née les coups de té
phone se succédèrent
le soir, chacun rép
dant avec enthousias
à cette invitation,
pouvait voir réunis
Daunou de nombre
effet, entourant Mm
seiller Commercial de
sol »... donne le pu
B.F., Antoine Biolatto
aire Général de l'A
nes », Georges Rose

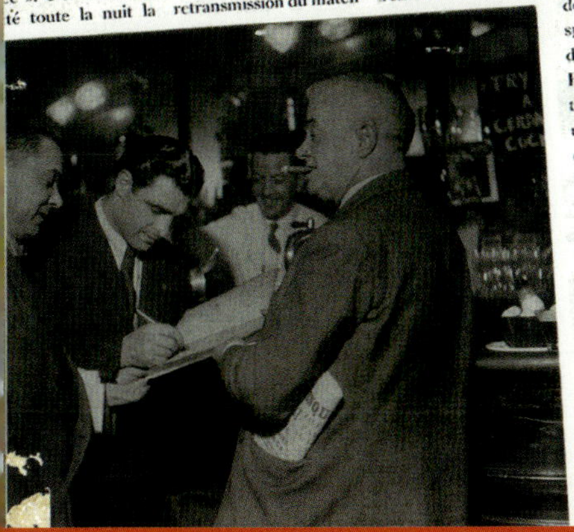

Marcel Cerdan (Mitte), Mittelgewichts-Weltmeister von 1948, signiert das Gästebuch von Harry's Bar, bevor einen »Cerdan Cocktail« trinkt.

Champion et lorsque l'on saura que ce « Cerdan ... comprendra aisément que si « Bartissol »... do
gnac Godet » avec une pointe de Sherry on comp'endra aisément que si « Bartissol »... do
punch, les invités de M. Pierre Bourut et du « Harry's New-York Bar » avaient, en sortant, le
... l'un ou l'autre.

BOXING BOXING

Saturday, December 7 - Velodrome d'Hiver

JEFF DICKSON Presents

PRIMO CARNERA

VS

YOUNG STRIBLING

Other high-class bouts. Secure seats in advance, at Harry's Bar, 5 Rue Daunou; Bank Tours, 3 Rue Auber; Jeff Dickson, 2 Rue Grétry; and general Agencies. Popular prices.

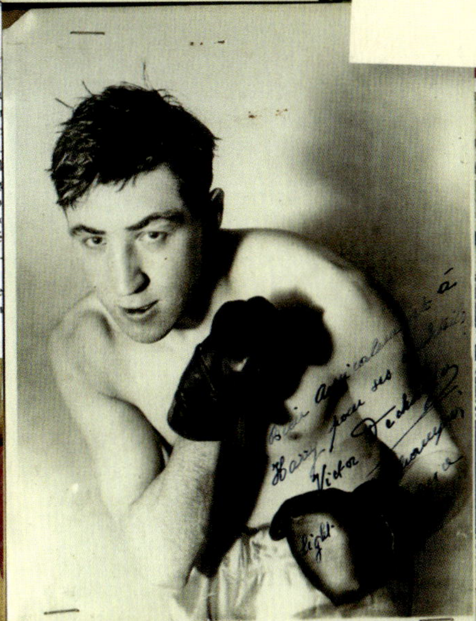

Harry's New-York Bar

KNOCK-OUT COCKTAIL

- 1/3 Gin
- 1/3 trockener Wermut
- 1/3 Absinth oder Anis
- 1 TL weißer Pfefferminzlikör

Schütteln und abseihen.

(Erfunden 1926 für Gene Tunney, als er Schwergewichts-Weltmeister wurde.)

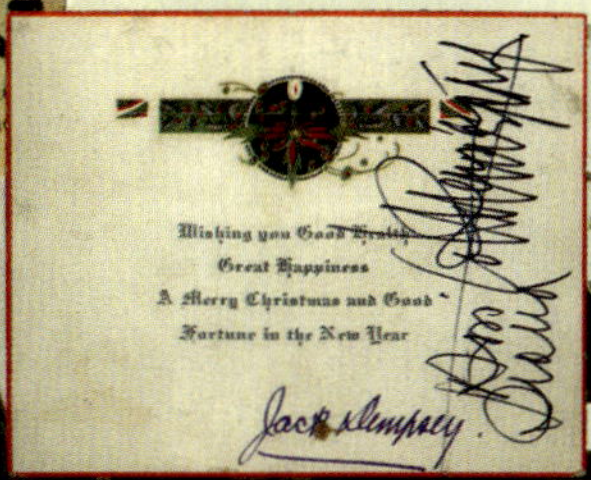

Primo Carnera (rechts) schenkt Harry 1933 nach dem Gewinn der Schwergewichts-Weltmeisterschaft seine Boxhandschuhe.

Harry's New-York Bar

WHISKEY SOUR

Im Shaker:

- 60 ml Bourbon Whiskey
- Saft ½ Zitrone
- Zucker nach Geschmack
- Schütteln und abseihen,
- mit einer Kirsche garnieren.

Andrew MacElhone: »Hemingway konnte 20 Whiskey Sour hintereinander wegkippen und dann in seinem Hotel wieder an die Arbeit gehen.«

WHO'S WHO IN HARRY'S BAR

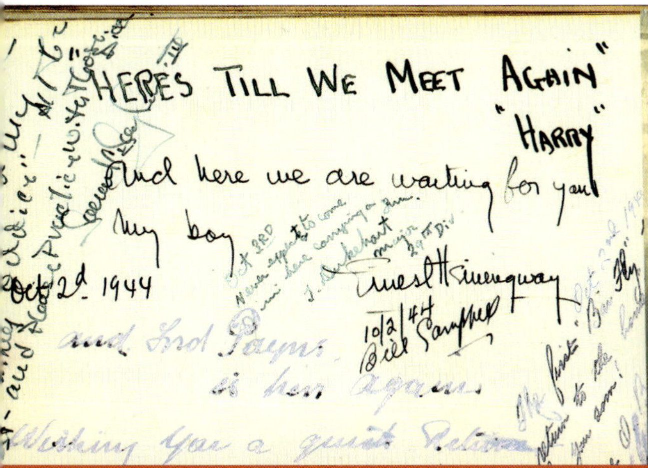

Am Ende des Zweiten Weltkriegs zeigte Harry sein Gästebuch, das er im Londoner Exil begonnen hatte, seiner Tochter Patricia. Sie kam gleich nach der Befreiung von Paris mit dem Roten Kreuz in die französische Hauptstadt und eröffnete Harry's Bar aufs neue.

ERNEST HEMINGWAY

Hemingway wurde am 21. Juli 1899 in Oak Park im Bundesstaat Illinois geboren. Er entdeckte schon früh die Kunst des Schreibens und wurde ein überragender Romancier. Mit 19 war er bereits Reporter beim *Kansas City Star*. Doch es zog ihn nach Europa. Also meldete er sich im Juni 1918 freiwillig als Krankenwagenfahrer in Paris und wurde anschließend Kriegsberichterstatter für die US-Presse. Harry's Bar betrat er das erste Mal im Jahr 1919 als junger Reporter, der gerade aus dem Krieg zurückkam. Harry's war eine seiner Lieblingsbars und er selbst eines der angesehensten Mitglieder des IBF. An seine Freundschaft mit Harry hatte er herzliche Erinnerungen. Harry seinerseits bewunderte diesen berühmten Trinker und ließ seinen Namen auf eine Metallplatte gravieren, die er an den Lieblings-Barhocker des Schriftstellers schraubte. Nach Ende des Zweiten Weltkriegs war Hemingway einer der ersten Amerikaner, die in die Bar zurückkamen, während Harry selbst sich noch in England aufhielt. Ab 1948 war Jack »Bumby« Hemingway, mit dem Andy einen Teil seiner Kindheit verbracht hatte, regelmäßig mit seinen Töchtern in der Bar zu Gast. Ernest Hemingway war viel auf Reisen und benutzte das Erlebte als Grundlage für seine Geschichten. Der Großteil seines Werks wurde zu seinen Lebzeiten veröffentlicht. Seine beste Arbeit ist zweifellos der Roman *Fiesta* – was sicher daran liegt, dass Harry's Bar darin vorkommt.

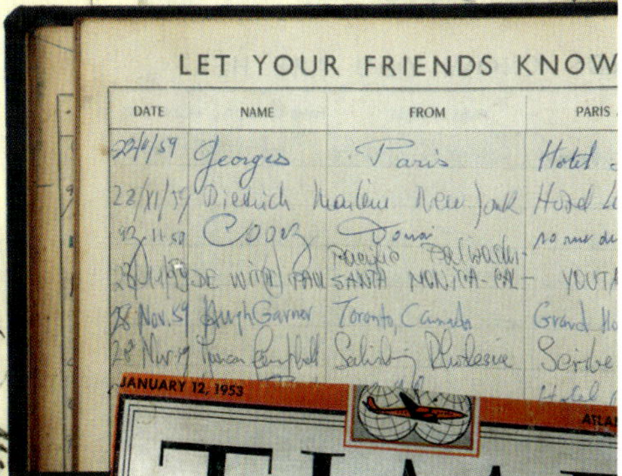

Freundschaftsbekundungen von Buster Keaton und dem Zirkusclown Emmett Leo Kelly (der sich in Cecil B. DeMilles Film Die größte Schau der Welt *selbst gespielt hat) sowie von Marlene Dietrich, Thornton Wilder, dem schottischen Varietékünstler und Schauspieler Will Fyffe und Jimmy Carter.*

LEFT BANK
RIGHT BANK
PARIS
AND
PARISIANS
By
Joseph A. Barry
H. Willard

Left Bank, Right Bank

transition, which brought out the work of Stein, Joyce, MacLeish, Crane and Kay Boyle, to mention a few— of it for the first time. Eugene Jolas, *transition*'s editor, back in Paris, because, he says, "The culture of the future is American, but you can see it better from Paris. There is a synthesis of occidental culture taking place in America, and Paris, as the intellectual capital of Europe, contributes to it. Ibsen and Joyce prove that a writer can live abroad and create the literature of his native country."

So far, however, if there is an unknown Fitzgerald among the younger writers in Paris, he remains unknown. After all, an unknown is an unknown. Several magazines have been attempted by Americans. One is dying of malnutrition, the other was stillborn. Right after the war I had formed a publishing house and advertised that I would read any and all manuscripts. What came in, alas, was unreadable.

Maybe there is someone writing quietly and steadily in some secluded, cold-water hotel room who will make me (gladly) swallow my words. But so far there has been no indication that the fifties will produce the same revolution in literature that the twenties and the lost generation produced. American writers in Paris today talk more of action than of art. The hundreds of American reporters, for instance, are much more political than literary and spend more time at their desks than at Harry's New York Bar on Rue Daunou. In the old days, Hemingway and Elliot Paul and the others would work on and off as journalists in order to earn the francs to pursue their own writing careers. Now reporting is a full-time, lifetime job. Indeed, one reporter, who used to publish short stories, says he can no longer write fiction, because his mind is wholly on "the factual things of politics."

The writers who come here seem gripped by the picture

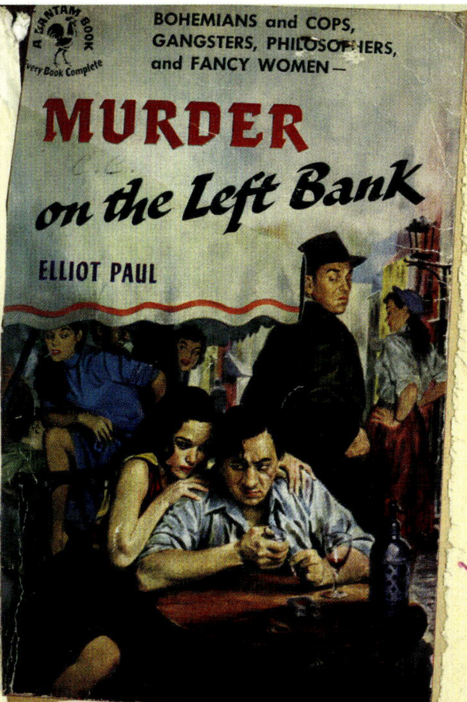

dinner of the voyage had been served and eaten; the final night was not to be like other nights at sea. Cherbourg would be sighted; then, at some eerie hour, the liner would nose behind the breakwater and inch up to the dock at Le Havre. Megan's dancing partner of that moment was a selectman of the town of Rockport, Mass., who had known her since she was a tot on the Cape Ann beaches. Selectman Parker had not crossed the Atlantic before.

Trunks and packing cases had been brought from the hold to the passageways and decks; cabin luggage was in heaps, in and outside of staterooms.

The young men were importunate enough that evening, but Megan danced a number of times with middle-aged men, because of what was stirring vaguely in her mind. Lieutenant Kitchel, who talked like a truck driver but who seemed to know everything two months before it was scheduled to happen, was expecting to meet a mature woman. The boys her own age—there were about twenty of them aboard, eight French, three assorted, and the rest Americans—seemed young and jejune. None of them, as far as she knew, had received prophetic mysterious letters, about which they could tell no one, or transoceanic telephone calls suggesting that they were to "get to" General or Prince de Gaulle.

"Where are you stopping, in Paree?" asked the Rockport selectman, Mr. Parker. "Your old man and I have promised ourselves to see the meat markets together."

"Meat markets!" Megan repeated. "Mother has mentioned only cathedrals, churches, museums, fairs, concerts, exhibitions and historical monuments."

"Meat markets, Harry's Bar, and the Folies Bergère," Selectman Parker insisted drily. "And some of those secret gambling dens around the Etoile."

"I want to meet Schiaparelli and Molyneux . . ." Megan began.

"That Molyneux murdered somebody years ago, didn't he? I'd forgot he got away," the selectman said.

It is better not to try to indicate how Megan and Mr. Parker pronounced the French words, but the distinguished French-

9

A. C. SEDGWICK

TELL SPARTA

To Harry,
In whose emporium
the idea for this book
was born.
And while we're at
it, best wishes
for a merry Christmas
& a swell New Year
Martin Fleer
Bob Korn

Tell Sparta 77—

station master's, told him who she was, and protested. The station master smiled at her indulgently, then started talking. The upshot of his frenzied discourse, she gathered, was that the press could make a government fall but with all its power it couldn't make an overloaded train arrive promptly—in wartime. Never.

Pearl remembered the many competent observers back from Nazi Germany who told her that everything ran like clockwork in the Third Reich, that Göring played with toy trains, that all he did was to press buttons to make them scurry in and out of tunnels—and how he pressed buttons too, to make little bombers take off to wipe out miniature cities. . . . Yet here, a French station master, in a real world, at real war, could do nothing better than make a speech at her.

Harry's New York Bar, she imagined, would be the fountainhead of all information this morning, but she wasn't sure she could count on getting there and back within three hours—in war. So, instead, she decided to eat at the station restaurant, which many gourmets incidentally (and there were quite a number of gourmets among newspaper men) had told her was one of the very best in Paris. Secretly, however, she yearned for just a cup of coffee and a lettuce-mayonnaise sandwich at a drugstore counter.

The spacious dark, sad Gare de Lyon restaurant was only fairly crowded. She was shown to a table for two. Sitting down she happened to push the plate aside. Underneath it she saw a slip of paper, torn out from a copy book. Obviously it had been planted there. In purple ink, scratched by a flimsy pen, such as you got in the Paris postoffices, she read, *'Pour quoi? Pour qui?'* and she studied the terrifying challenge, knowing just enough French to suspect what it meant. It gave her an idea for a lead to her story (if she didn't have to fall back upon the story already written by Betty Branish)—'Evidence of a strong Fifth Column exists in . . . Existed today tremendous evidence of subversive Fifth Column activity . . .' How lucky she was to have come to this particular restaurant!

She called the head waiter, because technique required you to get reaction on the spot. Wasn't this treason, now there was a war on? Shouldn't there follow wholesale arrests?

The headwaiter shrugged his shoulders.

DODSWORTH

a Novel by

SINCLAIR LEWIS

hb

HARCOURT, BRACE AND COMPANY

NEW YORK

142 DODSWORTH

with people who buzzed up and wanted to guide him, and l himself in impenetrable thoughts.

He roused himself to read, patiently, in Baedeker: "Ge frey Plantagenet, son of Henry II of England, was buri beneath the high altar in 1186. In 1430 Henry VI of Engla was crowned king of France and in 1560 Mary Stuart (aft ward Mary Queen of Scots) was crowned as queen-con of Francis II. The coronation of Napoleon I and Joseph de Beauharnais by Pope Pius VII (1804) . . . was celebra here with great ceremony."

(And in Saurier's studio brassy women were chatte about the races!)

Plantagenet! Rearing lions on scarlet banners edged bullion. Mary Stuart and her proud little head. Napol himself—here, where Sam Dodsworth was sitting.

"Humph!" he said.

He stared at the Rose Window, but he was seeing wha meant, not what it said. He saw life as something greater more exciting than food and a little sleep. He felt that he no longer merely a pedler of motor cars; he felt that could adventure into this Past about him—and possibly venture into the far more elusive Present. He saw, unha pily, that the Atkins and De Pénable existence into whi Fran had led him was not the realization of the "great lif for which he had yearned, but its very negation—the bust the little snobberies, the cheap little titles, the cheap litt patronage of "art."

"I'm going to get out of this town and do something— Something exciting. And I'll make her go with me! I've bee too weak with her," he said weakly.

His longing for low and intelligent company could not b denied. He went to the New York Bar. Through the co respondent of a New York newspaper whom he had know as a reporter in Zenith, Sam had met a dozen journalis there, and he felt at home with them. They did not heap o him the slightly patronizing compliments which he had fro the women in Madame de Pénable's den of celebrities. H was stimulated by what was to the journalists only commo place shop-talk: how Trotsky really got along with Stalin—

Il me fallait passer la semaine à Paris où allait se jouer une grosse partie de championnat le dimanche prochain. J'attendais Marie-Louise au *Harry's Bar* en rêvassant sous les gants suspendus de Primo Carnera. Carnera était un colosse italien, près de deux mètres, plus de cent vingt kilos. Il avait enlevé le titre de champion du monde de boxe toutes catégories, vers 1933, en mettant Jack Sharkey hors de combat à la sixième reprise. Par la suite, on avait raconté que les combats de Carnera étaient arrangés par des fumeurs de cigares. Le bon Primo n'en était pas moins resté pour son pays l'homme qui avait déchiqueté la légende de l'Italien exigu et fuyard.

Certains jours je passais rapidement entre le bar, tapissé des monnaies du monde dans leur version de papier, et les vitrines où dormaient des whiskies disparus depuis cinquante ans. Le *Harry's* était paisible l'après-midi et je pouvais m'y installer avec mes paperasses. Piombo venait bavarder un moment sous l'écusson d'une université américaine. Je me rappelle son étonnement un jour où, me cherchant au sous-sol où j'écoutais Charlie Lewis jouer du piano, il avait vu la photographie des cent mille spectateurs du match Carpentier-Dempsey et constaté que les indications pour les toilettes étaient fournies dans toutes les langues, y compris le grec et le latin.

— Je n'arrive pas à respecter les femmes qui font des manières. Aujourd'hui encore, j'éprouve une sorte de vénération pour Colette Ruisseau, tu te rappelles, je t'en ai souvent parlé à Lyon. Baba, très bien aussi. Pour moi sa promptitude efface sa légèreté. Quand je l'ai rencontrée *Aux Iles Marquises*, c'était le désert, la soif, l'eau saumâtre, les radeuses du faubourg Montmartre. Elle arrive, elle s'assied, elle me dit bonjour, et c'est tout de suite le plaisir. Tu comprends, tout de suite, dans la nuit même. Voilà la grande merveille. La multiplication de ses aventures, quand j'y pense, ne peut plus que m'amuser. Tandis que sa vitesse, eh bien, mon vieux, elle me donne encore chaud au cœur.

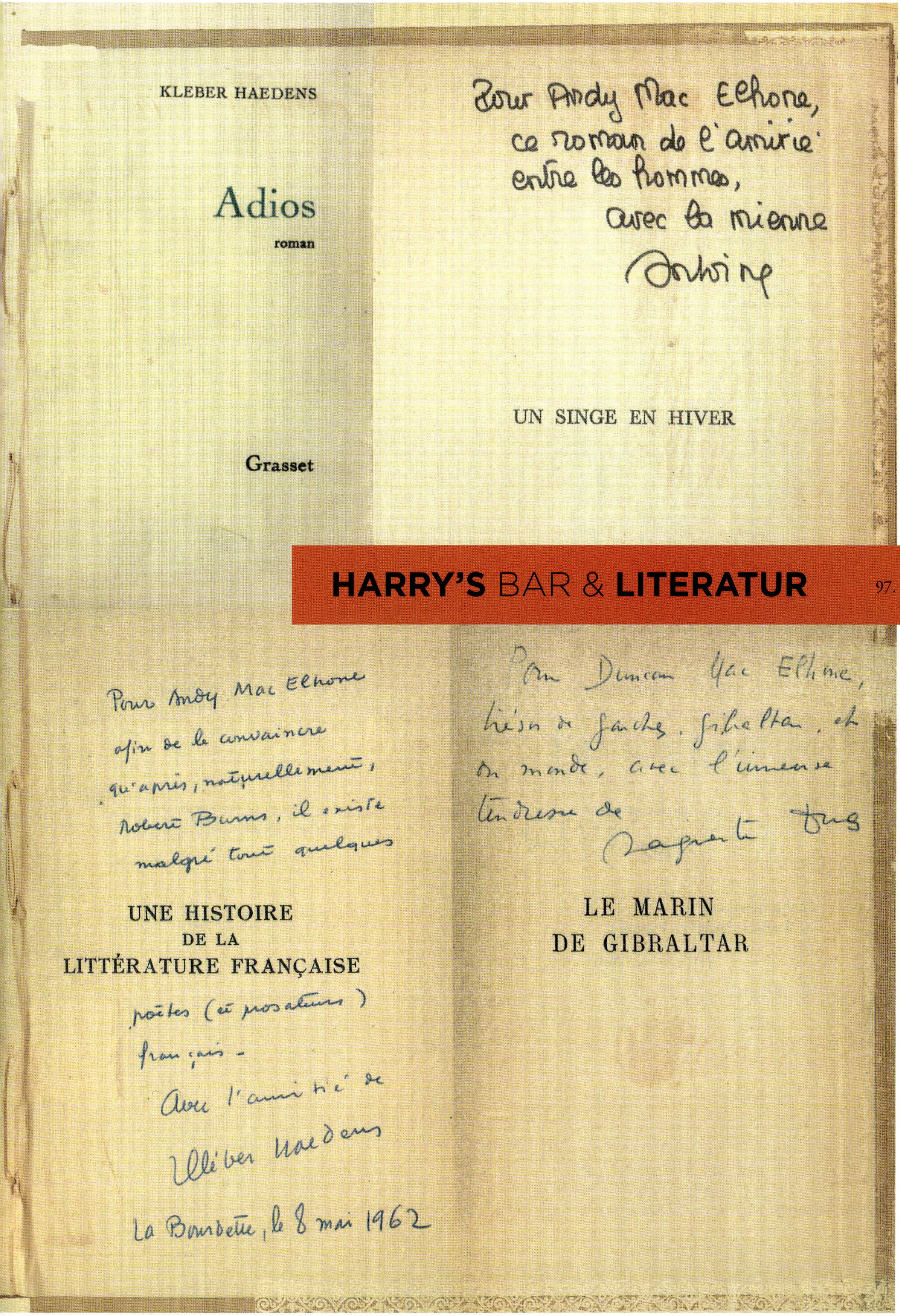
KLEBER HAEDENS
Adios
roman
Grasset
Pour Andy Mac Elhone,
ce roman de l'amitié
entre les hommes,
avec la mienne
Antoine
UN SINGE EN HIVER
Pour Andy Mac Elhone
afin de le convaincre
qu'après, naturellement,
Robert Burns, il existe
malgré tout quelques
UNE HISTOIRE
DE LA
LITTÉRATURE FRANÇAISE
poètes (et prosateurs)
français –
Avec l'amitié de
Kléber Haedens
La Bourdette, le 8 mai 1962
LE MARIN
DE GIBRALTAR

Gallup « de paille » dans un bar parisien

Rue Daunou, Paris : le quarante-neuvième État d'Amérique a voté

PARIS AMERICANS "VOTE" AT HARRY'S

The Rue Daunou emporium in Paris, which is known to every thirsty and homesick American throughout the world as "Harry's New York Bar" is the scene of much debating these days. Patrons are invited to express their preferences, and the results of the straw-vote, pretty close to date, are the subject of much comment. Yes, you've guessed it. The prosperous-looking gentleman with the cigar is Harry himself – Mr. McElhone to you.

Rou ACME, Paris, 10/27/36

VOTE
CTIONS

	307
ER	312

ARTIES NAMES

LES AMERICAINS DE PARIS VOTENT DANS LEUR BAR PREFERE

A CHAQUE ÉLECTION PRÉSIDENTIELLE LES PROPRIÉTAIRES DU HARRY'S BAR, QUI EST LE BAR PARISIEN PRÉFÉRÉ DE LA COLONIE AMÉRICAINE, ORGANISENT UN "VOTE POUR RIRE", (OU STRAW VOTE), ET LES RÉSULTATS SONT INSCRITS CHAQUE JOUR SUR LA GLACE PLACÉE DERRIÈRE LE COMPTOIR.

NPM: LES "ÉLECTEURS" DÉPOSANT LEUR BULLETIN DE VOTE DANS L'URNE POSÉE SUR LE COMPTOIR DU BAR.

RAT/JAC/061156– KEYSTONE

PARIS STRAW VOTE
PRESIDENTIAL ELECTIONS

H. TRUMAN A. A. BARKLEY	
H. WALLACE Glen TAYLOR	
T. DEWEY E. WARREN	

NOTE MARK YOUR **X** IN SQUARE OPPOSITE PARTIES NAMES

SIGN HERE: ....
HOME TOWN AND STATE: ....
REMARKS: ....

RESULTS WILL BE POSTED DAILY AT:
HARRY'S NEW YORK BAR
5, RUE DAUNOU (Opera District) – PARIS

PARIS STRAW VOTE
PRESIDENTIAL ELECTIONS

Gov. Adelai E. STEVENSON	
Gen. Dwight D. EISENHOVER	

NOTE MARK YOUR **X** IN SQUARE OPPOSITE PARTIES NAMES

SIGN HERE: ....
HOME TOWN AND STATE 1952

RESULTS WILL BE POSTED DAILY AT:
HARRY'S NEW YORK BAR
5, RUE DAUNOU (Opera District) – PARIS
JUST TELL TAXI DRIVER "SANK ROO DOE NOO"

Harry's New-York Bar

TLEVESOOR COCKTAIL

- Je 1 Spritzer Pfirsichbitter, Genever, Curacao
- $^1/_6$ Orangensaft
- $^1/_6$ Grapefruitsaft
- $^1/_3$ Roggenwhiskey
- $^1/_3$ Calvados

Gut schütteln und abseihen.

(Am 4. März 1933 in Harry's Bar in Paris von Bob Card erfunden, anlässlich der Amtseinführung von Präsident Roosevelt.)

Harry's New-York Bar

PRINCETON COCKTAIL

- 2 Spritzer Orangenbitter
- 1 Teelöffel Portwein
- 60 ml Gin

Gut schütteln und abseihen und eine Zitronenschale darüber ausdrücken.

HARVARD COCKTAIL

- ½ Cognac
- ½ süßer Martini
- 2 Spritzer Angostura
- 1 Spritzer Gomme-Sirup

Schütteln und abseihen.

L'HISTOIRE DU MONDE TOURNE UNE PAGE

INDICATIONS DE SERVICE (Contrôle de la transmission, collati...

= COL COCKTAILS +

Le télégramme est identifié à l'aide des indications portées, dans l'ordre c... avant le texte du télégramme. L'heure de dépôt est indiquée par un nombre ... chiffres.

ORIGINE	NUMÉRO	NOMBRE DE MOTS	DATE DE DÉPOT	HEURE DE DÉPOT	MENT...

PARIB F<≡25211TR PARIC F

<≡26211RD PARIB F

PARIS TELEXE DE MONTECARLO 025512 13 8 1425 =

CHALK UP TWO YANK VOTES FOR NIXON = LOUISE AND BOB SHEERIN

NIXON? KENNEDY?
COME & CAST YOUR STRAW VOTE AT
HARRY'S NEW YORK BAR
SANK ROO DOE NOO
Results posted daily.

HARRY'S

PARIS STRAW VOTE PRESIDENTIAL ELECTIONS

RICHARD M. NIXON	
JOHN F. KENNEDY	

Mark your **X** in square opposite your candidate's name

Sign Here :

Home town and State :

RESULTS will be posted daily at :

HARRY'S NEW YORK BAR

5, RUE DAUNOU (OPERA DISTRICT) PARIS

JUST TELL TAXI DRIVER "SANK ROO DOE NOO"

Von links nach rechts: Alain Pinto da Silva (Manager), Isabelle MacElhone (Geschäftsführerin), Franz-Arthur MacElhone (Urenkel).

Harry's New-York Bar

Ron Runer

The Bloody-Mary Man

High on the list of eye-openers which Americans will drink on New Year's Day is the Bloody Mary. But its popularity as a hangover remedy (page 49) still surprises **Fernand Petiot** of Canton, Ohio, the bartender credited with inventing the drink.

The year was 1920. The place was Paris and Harry's New York Bar. Bartender Petiot poured a can of tomato juice into an equal portion of vodka—and voilà: "We all agreed it was pretty good," recalls Petiot, a bald Frenchman whose accent is now a soothing 3:1 mixture of English and French. "One of the boys suggested we call it Bloody Mary," Petiot explains, "because the drink reminded him of the Bucket of Blood club in Chicago, and he had a girl named Mary."

Petiot brought the drink with him in 1934 when he came to New York to be head bartender at the St. Regis Hotel, a post he held for more than 30 years. There Petiot added seasoning because many New Yorkers considered it too flat. Petiot's perfected recipe: "Cover the bottom of the shaker with four large dashes of salt, two dashes of black pepper, two dashes of cayenne pepper and a layer of Worcestershire sauce. Then add a dash of lemon and some cracked ice, put in two ounces of 100-proof vodka and two ounces of thick tomato juice; shake, strain and pour." Recently retired and living in Canton (his wife's hometown), the 66-year-old Petiot tends bar part time ("to keep my hand in"), downs two scotch and sodas daily ("my favorite drink—it's safest") and buys only the best champagne for his New Year's toasting. Petiot doesn't see any new frontiers for bartenders to conquer. "Everything," he says, "has already been mixed together."

Newsweek, January 2, 1967

THE REBIRTH OF THE BLOODY MARY

In 1921, at Harry's New York Bar in Paris, France, a man named Fernand Petiot first mixed what was to become the famous Bloody Mary. (A few years later he became the head mixologist of the King Cole Bar in New York City. And here he introduced his drink to the fun-loving people of the roaring '20s.)

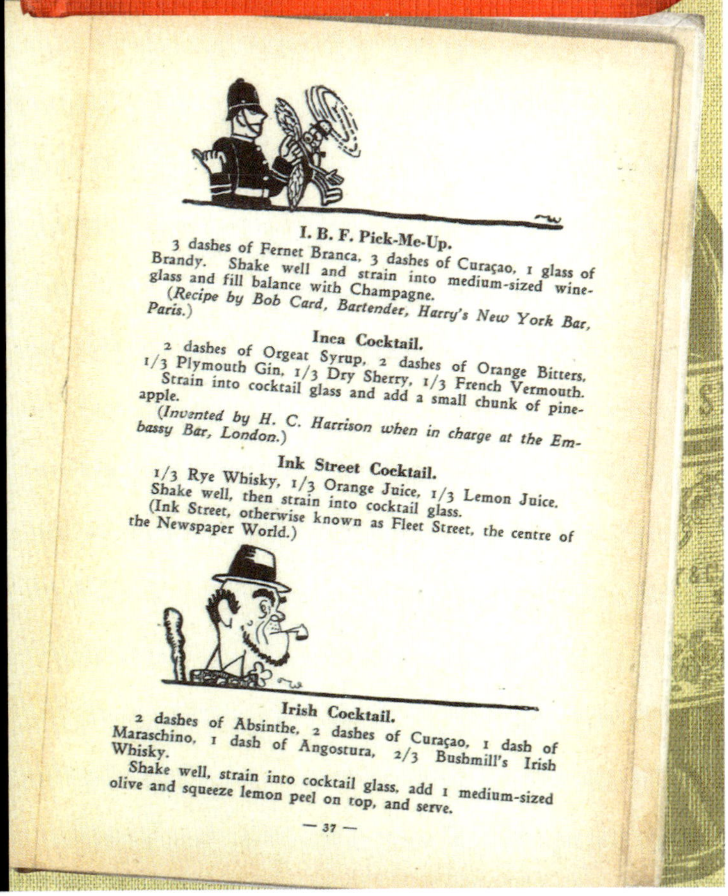

I. B. F. Pick-Me-Up.

3 dashes of Fernet Branca, 3 dashes of Curaçao, 1 glass of Brandy. Shake well and strain into medium-sized wine-glass and fill balance with Champagne.

(*Recipe by Bob Card, Bartender, Harry's New York Bar, Paris.*)

Inca Cocktail.

2 dashes of Orgeat Syrup, 2 dashes of Orange Bitters, 1/3 Plymouth Gin, 1/3 Dry Sherry, 1/3 French Vermouth. Strain into cocktail glass and add a small chunk of pine-apple.

(*Invented by H. C. Harrison when in charge at the Embassy Bar, London.*)

Ink Street Cocktail.

1/3 Rye Whisky, 1/3 Orange Juice, 1/3 Lemon Juice. Shake well, then strain into cocktail glass.

(Ink Street, otherwise known as Fleet Street, the centre of the Newspaper World.)

Irish Cocktail.

2 dashes of Absinthe, 2 dashes of Curaçao, 1 dash of Maraschino, 1 dash of Angostura, 2/3 Bushmill's Irish Whisky.

Shake well, strain into cocktail glass, add 1 medium-sized olive and squeeze lemon peel on top, and serve.

— 37 —

Andrew McElhone, late of the Ritz Hotel, now serving in the Intelligence Corps.

There's Only One Harry's...

...which Hemingway called second home, maintains **Harold Stephens,** *and that's Harry's in Paris.*

Harry's New York Bar in Paris is one of the most famous bars in the world. But then there are other Harry's Bars scattered around the world — in Venice, Florence, Los Angeles, Munich and a couple of other places. And each one, it seems, boasts that Ernest Hemingway had something to do with it. Who is right? Which is the original Harry's that Hemmingway knew so well?

I find myself very defensive on both subjects, Hemingway and Harry's. I grew up reading Hemingway — when he was still alive — and I was weaned standing at the bar in Harry's in Paris when Hemingway himself came charging through the swing doors and cigar-smoking Harry McElhone (the original Harry) was there to greet him.

But poor Ernest Hemingway would put on his boxing gloves and poke a few noses if he were alive to see what they are doing to his name and reputation, and so might old Harry if he knew how they are all cashing in on his bar in Paris.

For six straight years now, Harry's Bar & American Grill in Century City in Los Angeles has sponsored an "International Imitation Hemingway Competition" for aspiring writers. The catch is, the writing is supposed to be "bad" Hemingway instead of "good" Hemingway. So determined is Harry's Bar to capture publicity that the winner's prize is a trip to Florence, for two, and a dinner at Harry's Bar there.

The latest to get on the bandwagon is Sharky's Bar and Grill in Key West, Florida. They don't give prizes for writing contests there but they do sponsor a "Hemingway Look Alike

Photos by Harold Stephens

Against a backdrop of hundreds of autographed bills from all over the world, Andy McElhone sits, confident that only the unenlightened will doubt that Harry's began in Paris.

I absolutely refuse to be confused. So I went back to Harry's in Paris a few months ago to talk to Andy McElhone, who first tended bar for his father in the late 1940's.

With a refreshing lager in hand, a smiling Andy and I browsed through stacks of old photo albums and scrapbooks tucked away in back closets.

I was home, just as I had been in the 1940's when living in Paris meant, for

When the Bar first opened its doors on Thanksgiving Day in 1911, it was simply called "The New York Bar." It's founder was the famous jockey Tod Sloan who wanted to open a New York-type bar in Paris, even in the days before the American expatriates began arriving. To give it class, and authenticity, he had a West Side saloon dismantled and shipped piece by piece from New York to Paris. In a very short time it became a hangout for Americans in Paris.

During the dark days of 1914, the New York Bar was the meeting place for the Volunteers of the Lafayette Escadrille, and soon after it became unofficial headquarters for the American Field Service.

It was in 1919 when a young reporter named Ernest Hemingway first walked through the swing doors at Harry's. He had returned to Paris after the war with the intention of becoming a writer. Over the next few years he learned much of his trade from other literary giants while talking and arguing with them in Harry's.

When the 1920's roared in, Harry McElhone, a Scottish bartender who already had a reputation throughout Europe, bought the saloon and the name was changed to Harry's New York Bar.

Daily Mail Feature . ANDY ,Harry's son continuing to run the Bar . MANEVY .

KANSAS CITY STAR.

SECTION

KANSAS CITY, JULY 27, 1958—SUNDAY

STARBEAMS.

he Son of Harry the Scot, in Kansas City, Talks About His New York Bar—in Paris.

Harry's New-York Bar

K2 COCKTAIL

- **$^1/_3$ Wodka**
- **$^1/_3$ Zitronensaft**
- **$^1/_3$ Verveine du Velay (grün)**

Schütteln und in ein mit Rasureis gefülltes Glas abseihen.

(In Harry's Bar in Paris von Andrew MacElhone erfunden, als das französische Team bei der Besteigung des K2 1979 im Basislager eine »Harry's Bar« aufbaute.)

Paris 1977

A B C
of
MIXING
COCKTAILS

To Duncan;

This a book your grandfather Harry, wrote back in 1919 the first pages apply now just as much as they did then, & even more so, if you should ever want to follow his footsteps as mine in Bar work, not only learn them by heart, but follow them to the letter, let me wish you success & happyness in whatever you do

Andy

Andy and Duncan
take pleasure in inviting you
to celebrate

HARRY'S
75TH ANNIVERSARY

for which we thank you

November 30th at 5 PM.

R.S.V.P.
33 (1) 42617114

Sank Roo Doe Noo
5, rue Daunou - Paris
Cables: Cocktails, Paris

for the first time in 75 years
you will be welcome at Harry's Terrace

Tribune photo by Bob Fila

Andy [left] and Duncan MacElhone carry on a family tradition at Harry's New York Bar, now celebrating its 75th anniversary at 5 rue Daunou in Paris.

HARRY'S N.Y. BAR®

Falkenturmstraße 9
MÜNCHEN

M/S ASTOR
AT SEA

Geneva
Confederation Centre

Munich
9 Falkenturmstrasse

Montreux
Montreux Palace

Salzburg
The Point - Anif

Berlin
Grand Hôtel Esplanade

Montréal
Les Cours Mont Royal

L'EXPRESS
PARIS
Herald Tribune
BARS

Harry's New York Bar
HARRY'S
SANK ROO DOE NOO
Look out for these
Harry's

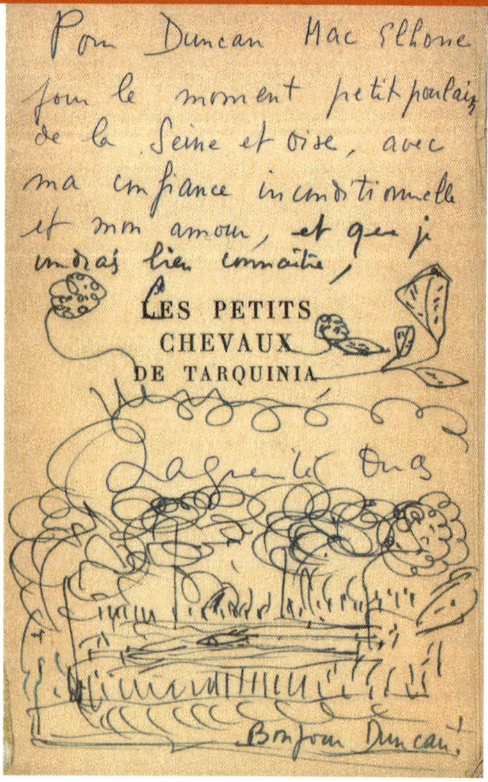
Pour Duncan Mac Elhone
pour le moment petit poulain
de la Seine et Oise, avec
ma confiance inconditionnelle
et mon amour, et que je
voudrais bien connaître,
LES PETITS
CHEVAUX
DE TARQUINIA
Bonjour Duncan!

entertainment
in the
Downstairs room
every
nite at the Ivories
To Duncan
good luck always
from his friend
Ernest Hemingway
Paris 1956-57

Harry's New-York Bar

LIBERTY COCKTAIL

- $1/3$ I. W. Harper Bourbon Whiskey
- $1/3$ trockener Martini
- $1/6$ Lime Juice Cordial
- $1/6$ Southern Mist

Schütteln und in ein Cocktailglas abseihen.

(In Harry's Bar in Paris von Duncan MacElhone erfunden für die französisch-amerikanische Gesellschaft zur Renovierung der Freiheitsstatue; bis zum 4. Juli 1986 ging ein Teil der Einnahmen an die Gesellschaft.)

Harry's New-York Bar

WELCOME STRANGER COCKTAIL

- $^{1}/_{6}$ Grenadine
- $^{1}/_{6}$ Zitronensaft
- $^{1}/_{6}$ Gin
- $^{1}/_{6}$ Schwedenpunsch
- $^{1}/_{6}$ Orangensaft
- $^{1}/_{6}$ Cognac

Schütteln und abseihen.

(1934 in Harry's Bar in Paris von Harry MacElhone erfunden.)

Le bar de Harry
le bar où j'ai ri
Tellement, tellement.
Petit coin de paradis
même un soir de rugby
J'y reviendrai avec
Jerome, Paul ou Henri...
chez Harry.

5.06.10.
Pas assez lucide pour écrire
un texte d'enfer... mais parfaitement
claire pour savoir que le Harry's
est un petit lieu magique hanté
par des êtres "maléfiques" (ou bien les
cocktails sont ...)
Merci Sylvie

Avis sur Harry's New York Bar le 20 avril 2010

★★★★★

Le Harry's New York Bar il faut y aller le temps d'une soirée électorale et là on comprend très vite que c'est le lieu de rdv de la communauté sur Paris :)

"Belle ambiance" ★★★★★ 20/02/2011

L'ambiance est plutôt du style "pub anglais" au Rdc et piano bar intime et chic au sous-sol. Un accueil de qualité et un fond musical tout en douceur font passer un très bon moment dans cet endroit qui vaut le détour.

Avis sur Harry's New York Bar le 5 juin 2009

★★★★☆

le temple du cocktails made in USA! plus de 200 cocktails et 150 whiskies vous y attendent.

Pour le Harry's
mon écriture ne vaut pas un clou
mais votre livre oui
La prochaine fois je trouve une tirade
drôle, promis
Vive le bar!
(Robinson)

110. MY HARRY'S BAR

02/10/10

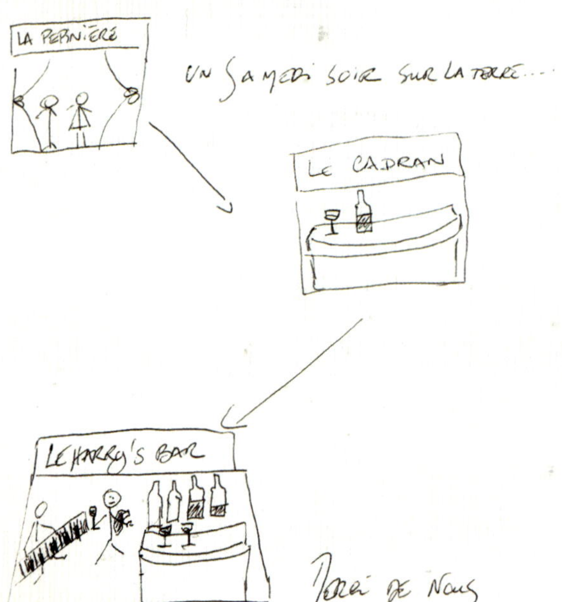

MERCI DE NOUS ACCUEILLIR SI CHALEUREUSEMENT...
ROMANE BOHRINGER

le, 23 août 2010
... alors,
pour le harry's bar
que j'aime beaucoup
et depuis longtemps...
mon père m'y emmenait
quand il avait gagné
aux courses...!
les barmen sont
formidables!
agnès
et merci pour Sarajevo

Le 10/05/10

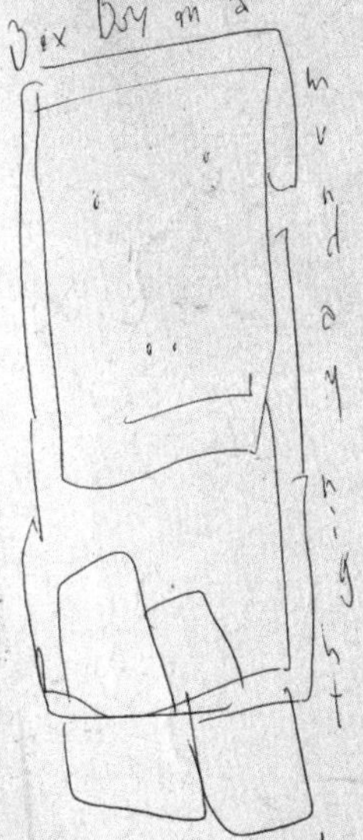

LOU DOILLON

Guy Montagné et
Pierre Bellemarre.

MEFIEZ VOUS
DES CONTREFAÇONS

Non

Je signe avec
plaisir sous ce
dessin de Guy
mon copain...
mon ami.
son admirateur

Bellemare

Ami Calmant
Guy Montagné

Cher Harry,

Tu me manques beaucoup depuis que j'ai pris la décision de refaire ma vie avec Jean-Pierre. En réalité c'est toi que j'aimais. Sois patient. Je reviendrai et nous serons heureux ENFIN. ENSEMBLE. Je le sais. Ô oui.

Ton Frédéric Beigbeder

le environ 18 août 2009 relativement tardivement.

Vétone Lavent

J'ai rencontré ce soir le charmant, inspirant et adorable Dzho. Il me parle de cet endroit et de son histoire que je ne connaissais pas. Je bois des mojitos en refaisant le monde et en parlant d'amours déçus. Et je me sens bien. C'est calme ici. Et j'ai l'impression d'être déjà venue en fait. J'aurais fumé des cigarettes mais il y a des lois maintenant dans ce pays. C'est pas grave. Je ferais avec un autre mojito!

Merci au Harry's Bar
pour ce merveilleux noir!

Love

Emmanuelle
Seigner

Merci Gilles!

112. **MY** HARRY'S BAR

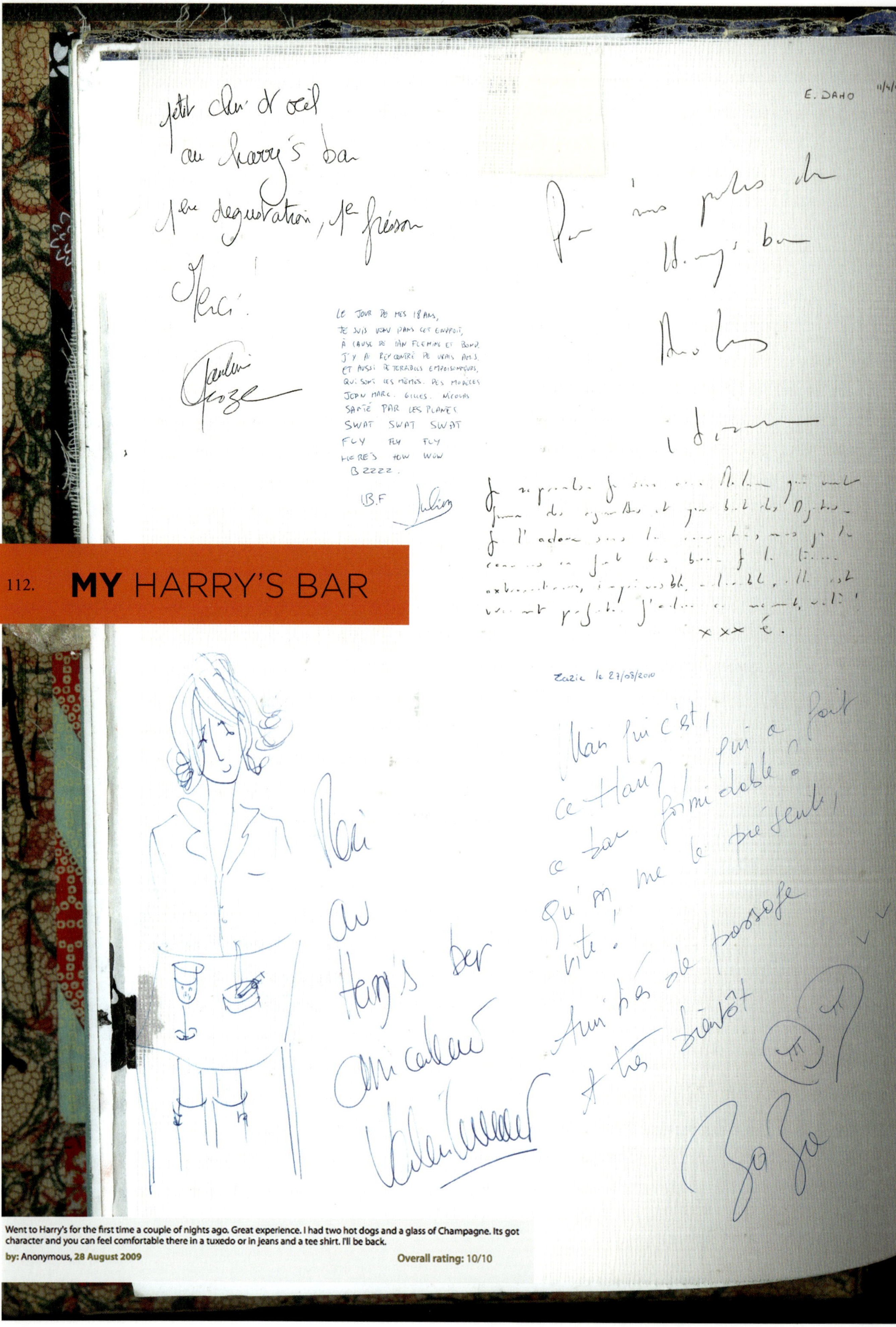

Went to Harry's for the first time a couple of nights ago. Great experience. I had two hot dogs and a glass of Champagne. Its got character and you can feel comfortable there in a tuxedo or in jeans and a tee shirt. I'll be back.

by: Anonymous, 28 August 2009 **Overall rating: 10/10**

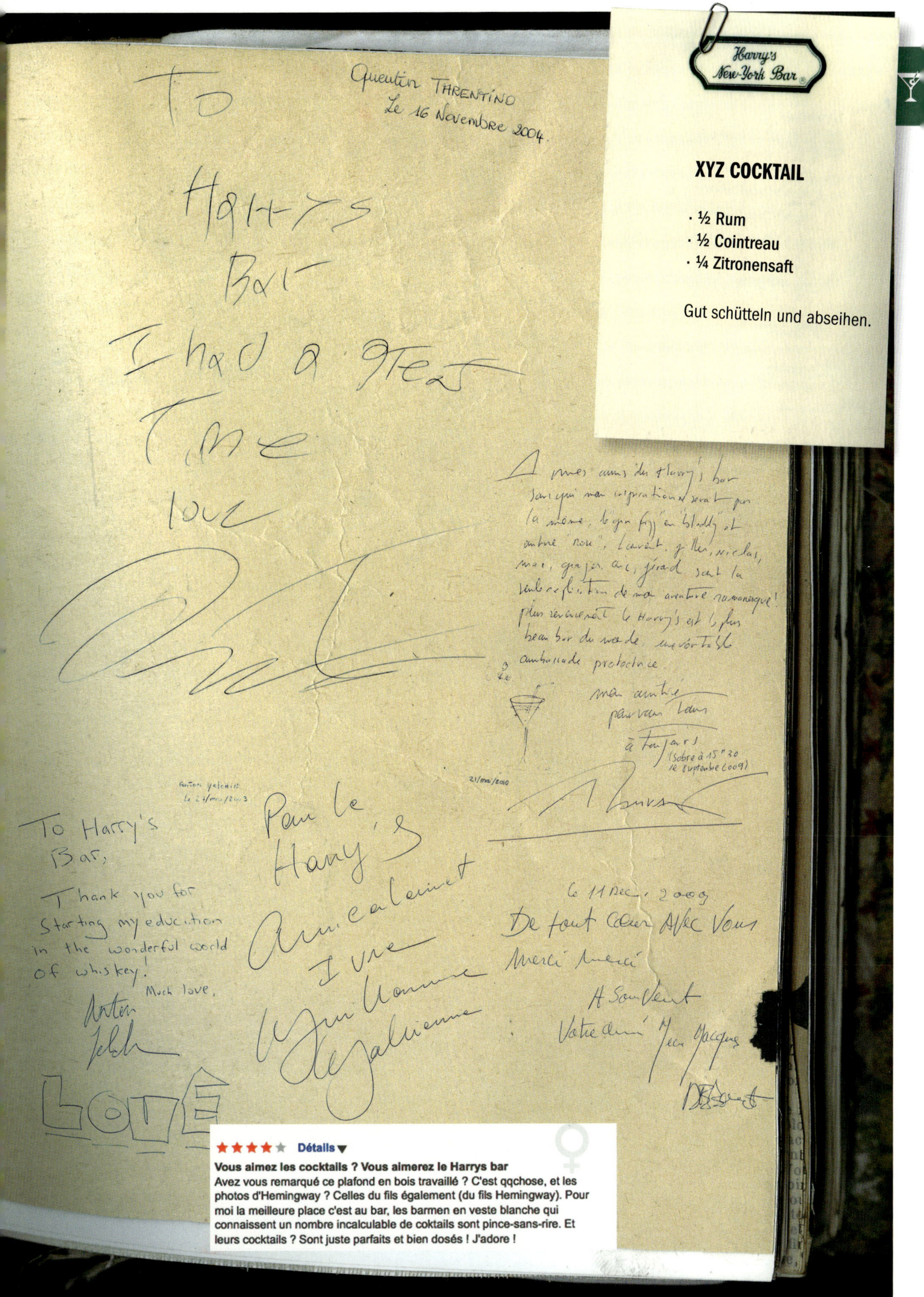

Harry's New-York Bar

XYZ COCKTAIL

- ½ Rum
- ½ Cointreau
- ¼ Zitronensaft

Gut schütteln und abseihen.

★★★★☆ Détails ▾

Vous aimez les cocktails ? Vous aimerez le Harrys bar
Avez vous remarqué ce plafond en bois travaillé ? C'est qqchose, et les photos d'Hemingway ? Celles du fils également (du fils Hemingway). Pour moi la meilleure place c'est au bar, les barmen en veste blanche qui connaissent un nombre incalculable de coktails sont pince-sans-rire. Et leurs cocktails ? Sont juste parfaits et bien dosés ! J'adore !

HOTS

STAR
D HOTS

BELLOWS
OLD FETTERCAIRN
MACALLAN
12
18
BOWMORE

CAOL ILA
BRUICHLADDICH
ISLAY
Ardbeg
MACNISH
GLENMORANGIE
Maker's Mark
WISCONSIN
NATIONAL CHAMPIONS
UMKC

K-STATE
ARIZONA
GEORGIA
entertainment
in the
Downstairs room
every

TULANE UNIVERSITY
PACIFIC
ASU

Das Privatarchiv von Harry's Bar / Harry's Bar »Personal Collection«

Layout / Design and layout: ★ **Bronx** Agence (Paris) – www.bronx.fr
Herausgeber, Bildbeschaffung und Seitenlayout / Publishing, Picture Research and Layout Manager: Anne Devanlay
Artdirektion / Artistic Director: Guillemette Gobbi
Bildrechte / Photo credits: Laurent Edeline / Bronx
Ohne die freundliche Unterstützung und Mitarbeit von Alain Devanlay wäre dieses Buch nicht entstanden. / This project could never have been completed without the friendship, authority and complicity of

Text von Isabelle MacElhone auf der Grundlage eines Manuskripts von Anne Devanlay (*Le Harry's Bar, Évolution d'une institution américaine de Paris de 1923 à 1958*, Paris-La Sorbonne, 1990) / **Text** by Isabelle MacElhone based on an original manuscript by Anne Devanlay (*Le Harry's Bar, Évolution d'une institution américaine de Paris de 1923 à 1958*, Paris-La Sorbonne, 1990)
Übersetzung / Translation: Geronimo Translations
Korrektur / Proof reader: Anne-Marie Valet

Bildrechte: Sämtliche Dokumente, Fotos, Autographe, Pressebilder, Zeitungsausschnitte, Zeichnungen, Karikaturen usw. aus dem Archiv von Harry's New York Bar. / **Photo credits and illustrations:** All documents, photos, signed photos, press photos, news copy and newspaper and magazine articles, sketches, caricatures, literary excerpts, autographs, etc. are from the *Personal Collection* in the Harry's New York Bar archive.
Harry's New York Bar dankt / Le Harry's New York Bar thanks: Acme News Picture, AFP, Agence Intercontinentale, Keystone View Company, Keystone Paris, Art Buchwald, Associated Press, Associated Press (Foto Jacques Brinon), C. Dugied, Chris Kindahl, *Daily Mail*, Ferrier (Dundee), France Éclair, International Sport (Foto Charles Dickson), Jean-Michel Vogue, *L'Express*, M. Piquemal, M.T. Bonney, *Elle*, *Life* (photo Yale Joël), Masséna Photo, Maurice Jarnoux (France Photo Illustration), Maurice Rougemont, *Newsweek - Paris-Match, Paris-Midi*, Photo Tscherniak, Photographie Industrielle Sartony, Pictoral Press, Ralph Starkweather, Robert Delhay, Russel Westwood, Taken 1928, *The New Yorker*, United Press Photos, Universal-Transcontinental-Films (photo Raymond Voinquel), Wide Word Photos, World Copyright (I. Kitrosser et autres associés).

Autorin und Verlag waren bemüht, die Rechteinhaber sämtlicher in diesem Buch veröffentlichter Abbildungen zu ermitteln. Sollte uns dies im einen oder anderen Fall nicht gelungen sein, bitten wir um Entschuldigung. / The publisher has made every effort to identify the photo credits of the images used in the present book. We apologize to anyone whom we have been unable to contact or identify if their name is missing from the credits.

Titel der Originalausgabe: *Harry's Bar*
Erschienen bei Éditions de La Martinière SA, Paris 2011

Deutsche Erstausgabe

Ein Unternehmen der La Martinière Groupe

Übersetzung für die deutsche Ausgabe: Claire Roth, London
Lektorat, Satz und Herstellung der deutschen Ausgabe: VerlagsService Dr. Helmut Neuberger & Karl Schaumann GmbH, Heimstetten

Druck: Imprimerie Pollina - L58545B
Printed in France

ISBN 978-3-86873-434-8

www.knesebeck-verlag.de